The Ascendence of
LOVE

Awakening to the Reality of Oneness

Anne Olsson

Copyright © Anne Olsson
Author and Publisher

First edition printed October 2024
Revised edition printed September 2025

To order copies of The Ascendence of Love please email:
thegentleheart@gmail.com

The right of Anne Olsson to be identified as the author of this work has been asserted by her in accordance with the Copyright, Designs and Patents act. All rights reserved. No part of this publication may be reproduced, stored in or introduced into a retrieval system, or transmitted, in any form, or by any means (electronic, mechanical, photocopying, recording or otherwise) without the prior written permission of the publisher.

ISBN: 978-1-7637324-1-4

Proudly produced by

TheBookStudio
www.thebookstudio.com.au

CONTENTS

Introduction..iv
Acknowledgements..vi

1. The Higher Path..................................1
2. At Rest in Stillness............................7
3. The Voice of Wisdom.......................13
4. The Pillar of Trust............................19
5. The Call for Love.............................27
6. Restoration of Vision.......................33
7. The Light of Truth...........................39
8. The End of Days..............................45
9. The Reality of Innocence................53
10. Transcendence.................................59
11. The Nature of Desire.......................67
12. The Flight of the Eagle....................73
13. God's Child is Sinless.....................81
14. Awakening......................................89
15. The End of Suffering......................97
16. The Pathway of Remembrance....................105
17. Freedom from Illusion..................113
18. Your Infinite Potential..................121
19. The Wisdom of the Body..............127
20. The Breath of Life.........................135
21. The Illusion of Time......................141
22. In the Quiet of the Forest..............147
23. Oneness..155
24. Freedom.......................................161
25. A Sense of Wonder.......................167
26. Truth Is..175
27. The Joy of Being...........................181

──── **Introduction** ────

When I rest in stillness, the words that I have scribed in *The Ascendence of Love* have quietly dropped into my mind. When I first began to record these messages from Jeshua, I questioned their veracity. As I became aware of the great wisdom and love inherent within them, I felt a growing sense of awe and learned to trust in what I was experiencing. Jeshua has been my beloved teacher and friend for decades now. When I feel his presence with me, I am deeply comforted. He has told me that it does not matter how I refer to him, because what is a name but a label that separates. It truly does not matter from whence these messages come. What matters is whether the power and wisdom of the words touch the heart of the reader. I have been assured that the book will reach those who will gain the most benefit from it, and this is all I could ask for.

As Jeshua has declared, words are inadequate to describe the truth. Truth is beyond description. Words are limiting, and at best they can only point towards the Truth. The Truth, however, can be felt. It is my prayer that you will feel the presence of Truth in the pages of this book. Initially, as I scribed the early chapters of this book, I felt uncertain about the repetition of major themes. While I was assured that the message of Love was paramount, I was told that our belief in separation was powerful, and the ego has resisted the truth that there is only One. 'All repetition is deliberate. The egoic mind is defensive against the truth so there is need for constant repetition to allow these words that we offer you to find a home in the mind. Because your resistance has been strong, it has been necessary to bring the truth of Oneness into your awareness gradually and persistently.'

Jeshua has been my loving guide and my comforter since I first began recording his words. Whenever I am anxious or uncertain,

I can turn to him for solace and reassurance. His words enter my awareness whenever I rest in the stillness and request his guidance. He counsels me when I am unable to find a solution to a problem or have misperceived a situation. I am deeply grateful for his presence in my life. I am in awe of the power of his love and the wisdom of his words. He frequently reminds me that he is never far from me: 'I am never apart from you. Even when you have no thought of me, I am with you. Through all the dramas and fears that beset you, I am with you, a very part of your Self.' As the scribe of these messages, I have been blessed by the insights with which he has gifted me, and pray that you too will find beauty, peace and understanding in his teachings.

As you travel steadily through your days, may you always be blessed with wisdom and uplifted by the power of the Truth. May you feel the peace of our Father's presence within you always and freely extend the Love that you are to all. May you trust in all that is and relinquish your fears and uncertainties to the One God, the One Light, the One Life.

Acknowledgements

It is with deep appreciation that I want to thank all those who have assisted me in bringing this book into publication, in particular James Willis and Liam Douglas. My sincere gratitude is extended to all my beloved Queensland friends who have listened to readings of the chapters and offered me encouragement during the writing of this book and *Surrender to the Stillness*.

I want to acknowledge the contribution of my friend Frances Robertson who edited early chapters of the manuscript. I have been blessed by her love and friendship and have appreciated her broad experience and sound editorial skills.

I deeply grateful to my beloved brother and teacher Jeshua for the gift of the words he has dropped into my mind. I am inspired by the insights he has offered me and the great love he has continually extended to me. I cannot adequately express to you the wonder and joy that his presence in my life has brought me.

The Higher Path

We come once again to speak of the power of Love and the illusion that fear is. Love is on the ascendance and the Earth is coming of age, asserting her independence from the past and the thought patterns destructive to her well-being. It is time for you to step into your power and embrace the Truth of who you are. The days of the ego are numbered. Love is rising in the consciousness of God's children and will not be gainsaid.

Beloved brothers and sisters, the time of awakening is here. The old ways of judgement and projection, blame and discord, are finally coming to an end. The vibration of the planet is rising. I come to assure you that all is well. This world that seems so real remains a dream. It has no reality. You remain as you were created to be. You are pure spirit, pure conscious awareness. You are made in the image of the Holy Father, eternal, unchangeable, limitless and free.

Because in Truth there is nothing outside of you, this world you experience is not outside of you. All events are neutral – *all* events – no matter what the ego may perceive. What does this mean? No event is inherently good or bad, right or wrong. It simply is what it is. The planet is seen to be experiencing discord and disharmony, and weather patterns changing dramatically. Institutions built on a foundation of fear are observed to be floundering, but do not doubt that there is nothing to fear. There is an intricate pattern of energies dancing and flowing to the rhythm of the divine orchestra and the Light of the Father's Love will reveal the stepping stones that will guide you through the coming days.

Precious friends, know there is nothing wrong. All is indeed well. There are no accidents in Creation and you do not have to change anything. You do not have to fix the world but simply change your mind about it. Why? Because it is your projection. And because it is your projection, this is the only way to fix it. Your mind is the cause of the world. You have dreamt up scenes of drama and discord, poverty and pain, but it is always a reflection of what is held in the mind. Only Love is real, and because you are Love, the *essence* of all you see is an extension of the Father's Love. Love is the foundation of the world. But until you are totally committed to being the presence of Love in every moment, until all fear is banished from your mind, you will still project images of fear outwards.

Enter into the silence often now and heed the Voice of the Comforter. It will guide you through every situation. Know that there is nothing to fear, nothing to hide from and nothing to fight against. Reality can never be threatened. Choose to love and abandon the false prophets of fear. No one else can make this decision for you. Why cling to old concepts that no longer serve you? False hopes will not serve you now. Only Love will serve you as you bid farewell to the world that taught you that illusions were real and Reality a fanciful dream.

Your world is waking up, and yet it seems that darkness is shrouding your planet and evil is rife. But indeed, it is the very presence of the wars and discord and seeming selfishness that is pointing to the forces of Love at work amongst you all. Love is the great power that will heal this planet, and it is Love that is stirring up the dark sediment that lies in the depths of those governed by fear. Fear is not an enemy. It remains an illusion. Abide now in the truth that even in the midst of the problems that beset this world,

Chapter 1: The Higher Path

Love is at the heart of all you see. Love is working to change, to heal, to soothe, to cherish all. Love is simply coming home to Itself. Oneness is waking up to Itself.

As changes occur in the world around you, you can maintain a deep trust in all that is happening. Your presence can be a haven of love, peace, and sanity when others are struggling in the darkness of fearful thoughts of their own creation. There is nothing to fear now, nor has there ever been anything to fear. There never will be anything to fear. The Son of God is safe. Only as he becomes lost in the morass of his own anxious thoughts and strives – and fails – to control events he perceives as fearful will he lose his way. But the Truth has never wavered. All is well. You are not a body. You are pure spirit, the child of the Holy Father who looks upon you and sees only the Love that you are.

I have said that fear is not your enemy, because you have no enemies. You can befriend fear, and it will have much to teach you. All the emotions that wash through you, you have branded as 'good' or 'bad', wanted or unwanted. You have judged them. We encourage you to simply allow them. And what does it mean to allow? It is to let all be as it is. To let go and trust. To let go of all the frantic gripping onto things that you hope will save you. To let go and let God. To dive into the abyss. To cut away all the strings that have held in place your concept of who you are. To abandon your beliefs in all you hold dear.

Does this seem extreme? To abandon all your beliefs in what you hold dear? Question your motives for clinging to those concepts that have been the pillars of your world. Question your belief in 'need'. Question your desire for security. Question your avoidance of all you have judged as unpleasant, harmful or disgusting. For what disgusts you? It is time to open your arms to all of life – to the ugliness and the pain, the cruelties and the dishonesties. Accept the human experience for what it is, in all its shades of lightness and dark. For how can you know joy if you shut yourself away from its brothers, the feelings of hatred and anguish and fear?

All must be tasted in their fullness so that you can walk free into the new world with all the old baggage cast from you and expelled from the cells of the body. You have suffered from emotional constipation and have sought an emotional laxative to set yourself free. You do not need this. You can walk free right now if you would let go all your grasping at straws that you hope will keep you safe. You do not need this because you are already safe.

We have told you that there is nothing wrong. We encourage you now to abandon all concept of wrongdoing, all notion of evil. These are not helpful. They are a recipe for fear. We call on you to remember the truth of every one of God's creations. Do not be deceived by what the media presents. Remember who you are and who your brother is. If you get caught up in the dramas that appear to be playing out around your world, you will lose yourself in a wilderness of confusion. Whenever you judge another as evil, you do but judge yourself and rob yourself of peace. The concept of evil is a creation of the ego and remains an illusion. Look beyond the confusion manifesting in your dream world and look into the heart of Love. Remember that Love allows and embraces all things, and thus transcends all things.

You are not living your life. You are being lived. The power of God is living and breathing as you. Beloved brothers and sisters, relinquish all concept of being in control. Let go of *trying* to do anything. Let go and let God live through you. Give up all attempts to guide the course of your life, and then you will have no need to strive or struggle, to seek gain or find direction. Life will become simpler, quieter and happier. The Love that you are will shine forth unimpeded.

Your minds are so powerful that any perception that there is something, anything, amiss will reinforce that belief in yourself and buttress negative energies acting on the planet. It is important to *know* that all is well now. This will be the most helpful act you can perform. Any perception that war, for example, is harmful and induces suffering is a thought form that will strengthen both the belief in war and the possibility of war arising on the planet. Come to accept the great power of mind that you hold and use it wisely. Do not believe in what your televisions depict. Do not convince yourself of the suffering of mankind. When you do, you are supporting a belief that fosters the rise of suffering. This is why we continually remind you that *all* is well always. Only this understanding will draw your brothers and sisters out of the nightmares they have created.

Now it is time to relinquish all fear, particularly of death. The spirit is eternal and incapable of experiencing death. The spirit remains indestructible. When a body perishes and the spirit leaves this world, there is in Truth nothing to fear and nothing for which to grieve. The body has been renounced but the spirit is unchanging and is without beginning and without end, ever one with the Father. God's Creation is One. When you look out upon the world and see the scenes of geographical upheavals and observe the effects of extreme weather events, be assured that there is no need for anxiety. All continues to be well. The dream remains a dream.

Beloveds, allow all to be as it is. Trust in the divine interplay of energies. Only Love is real, and life is ever the expression of the Love that the Father is. Suffering is not necessary, or in Truth even possible. The natural world does not suffer. If a plant dies, its cells will break down and feed the soil in which a seed lies dormant. With the coming of sweet rain, the seed will sprout, and new life will grow from the remnants of the old – for life on this planet is a dance of energies that ebb and flow with Divine Grace.

There is no separation. The Oneness you seek is inherent in all things. Because you and Mother Earth are One, she is mirroring your journey of awakening. There is only One: One Life,

One Consciousness, One Creation. If you can let go all sense of separation, you will begin to see the great beauty and intelligence that is crafting the interplay of life on this planet. The Power and Majesty of the Father is great and glorious and is made manifest in all that you see.

In Truth not one leaf can fall from a tree that will not be felt by the whole of Creation. You are not separate from your Father, or from your brothers and sisters. Every thought that makes its home in the mind of a brother or sister sends forth ripples into the minds of all God's children. Why is this of significance now? Because the earth changes and the human dramas being enacted are giving rise to anxiety. You are asked to rest in the truth that is always true. Let no fearful thoughts control your actions, and thus become a sanctuary of quietness and sanity.

Those who seek to run from their fears are simply running from themselves. Those who deny responsibility for what they experience will not be shielded from their own thoughts. Those who are willing to accept and trust all that they perceive will rest in the peace that is the Father's gift to those who realise that His Love is inherent in all that is occurring.

All that is taking place within the dream *is* in your best interests. There is nothing to fear. Everything is being enacted for you, not to you. Allow all to unfold according to the Divine Will, and trust in the Love that is alive in every moment and in every event. You are a manifestation of God's Love in form. The Father's Love is expressing as you and through you. Trust that Love is at the heart of all that is occurring, now and always. You remain as you were created to be. You are Christ, and you are eternal, limitless and free. Nothing can harm you. Fear is an illusion. Nothing real can be endangered. There is only God. Embrace this truth and peace will find its natural home in your consciousness.

Rest in Stillness

Beloved friends, these words come to you from the depths of who you are, where we are joined as One. For indeed we are One, inseparable from our Father. This moment of our sharing is precious. It is sacred. It is a holy moment in which to remember what is true. It is of God, because all is of God. And in this sacred moment know deep in your heart that Love is on the ascendance in your world, and all is well.

The time is ripe for transformation. Love is rising in the hearts and minds of men. Let Truth be your guide now. Become a flag-bearer who upholds the banner of trust and harmony, simplicity and concordance. These are the qualities of character that will serve you now and lead you along the path of peace. Man must now look deeply within himself and cast out the painful memories of the past and all notion of victimhood. He is not a victim of anyone or anything. This world and all the suffering that it has engendered yet remains a dream. Only by awakening to the reality of Love will the painful dream be dissolved.

Precious friends, I call on you now to set aside time as often as you can throughout your day, to be still and abide quietly in the truth of your being as Christ. Rest in the stillness and enter the silence that is ever-present beneath the clamour of busy thoughts and the noise and bustle of the outside world. Sink deeply into depths of this silence and peace will find you easily and naturally.

When you sit in the silence, do not have any expectations. Do not think this experience should be anything other than what it is. Know that all is well. Do not think you must sink into some deep place beyond this world that is all ethereal peace and light. This is not what we are asking of you. This is an exercise in allowance and surrender. Merely allow this time of stillness to be just what it is. Do not anticipate anything. Sit quietly, and rest into the moment and allow - without judgement. Be that which you are. And what does this mean? It means to allow yourself to be yourself in that time, even if thoughts run rampant and the body does not relax. Let it be what it is.

When you let go all expectations and self-judgement, you will find it easier to discover the peace that always lies within. There is no need to strive for peace. You need simply trust in the quietness, and rest gently into the moment. Allow all thoughts of your daily concerns to drift away. Give no heed to what is going on beyond you. Just let go all attempts to control or achieve anything. Allow all to be as it is and surrender to the silence. I will join you there, for in this place we are One. Here you will find solace and peace. Here your wounded spirits will be healed. Here you will find your Self.

Although many have consciously sought noise and activity to find distraction from the distress and confusion they feel, this only serves to mask the true Self. Yet the joy of inner tranquillity will lead you beyond all suffering. If you are willing to rest often in the inner silence, you will discover the peace that is your heritage. Because here there is no disharmony, no judgement, and no discord. Here there is only peace.

Join with me now and come with open hands and an open heart into the silence within. Do not bring anything with you. Leave behind your confusions, your so-called problems, your uncertainties, your doubts and all your grievances. They have no place here with me in this quiet place of peace and certainty. Here there are no stories from the past that would tell of dramas and discords. Here there is only Love. Here we can rest in the silence of eternity, in the precious stillness where all strivings have ceased, and all seeking has ended.

Rest here with me now, knowing that we are One. Rest with me and sink even deeper into this quiet place of peace and tranquillity and feel the presence of God. You will not find it in your worries or your questioning or your restlessness. It is to be found here in this sacred silence where the things of this world have faded from your awareness, and you have been caressed by the Grace of God.

Feel my presence with you as we kneel at the feet of our Father, washed by the sweet joy of His Infinite Love. Grasp my hand in recognition of our union and simply be. Here there is nothing to search for, for all that you hunger for has been offered to you. All you crave rests in the heart as it opens in the precious stillness of the Father's Presence. In ecstatic joy, let the riches of the heart flow freely outwards to offer Love to all.

The power of this process will become evident as you commit to resting in the silence daily. Simply rest, without agendas, without struggle, without analysing; simply rest, and discover this peace that is beyond all understanding. Why do we emphasise this process? Because this will comfort you and support you when events challenge your peace. Commit to doing this regularly, and it will bring you rewards that you cannot now conceive.

As you rest in the quiet, as you abide in the truth of who you are, know that this time is sacred. It is a gift from your Self to yourself. It is the dawn of awakening itself. As you rest in the stillness, let this peace come to you quietly, gently dismantling the structures of thought the egoic mind has constructed to protect itself from illusory dangers. Here, in the quiet places of the Heart, Love reigns and will show you the absurdity of all fear. Here in the deep recesses of your being, the song of joy can be heard, as a choir of angels heralding the end of all illusions and the awakening of Christ from his long slumber.

Now, as these words enter your awareness, remember that only Love is real. You are the essence of Love, and all the emotions that colour your experience in this world cannot mask the Truth of who you are as Love. Relax into this awareness now. *Only Love is real*. All that is born of fear is simply the creation of the ego and is an illusion of mind. The Father knows nothing of fear. He is Love Itself, and ever extends the Love that He is outwards to His creations.

As you abide here in this moment, feel this love within you... Rest quietly now, and breathe deeply... In this stillness, feel this love that is your essence. Allow it to extend outwards.... The world is crying out for love now. Feel your love radiating out to Mother Earth, embracing her and bringing her sustenance. Know that her heart will open to receive this love... Sense a softening come upon you, a surrendering into the Truth that is eternally true. Each time you make this offering, you present a precious gift to the planet.

Let Love be your focus and your motivation now. Let it guide you along every pathway, and around every obstacle to peace. Question your every action: 'What is truly motivating my experience now?' Because if you are not at peace, you have chosen to be fearful. You have decided that fear is what you want, and that fear will bring you to where you want to go and what you would receive. But fear will not set you free. It will only lead you deeper into the mire of false perceptions and tumultuous emotions. Only peace will satisfy the yearnings of your soul now, and only Love will lead you to peace.

Beloved brothers and sisters, when you abide in the stillness and feel the presence of the Father's Love that surrounds you and penetrates you, know that it illuminates every cell of the body, and everything you look upon. It is Love itself that allows you to think and feel. It is Love that manifests as the dance and play of energies that appear to you as your world of bodies and solid objects. If you can become aware of the force of love within you and feel its power to bring harmony to your world, you will be able to wield this love as a blade to cut through the walls of false concepts and the dark and ugly structures of attack and defence built by fear.

If fear cries out 'I am lost,' Love will find you and bring you home. If fear condemns an event as sinful or dangerous, Love will assure you that you are safe and that all is well. If fear would cause you to point your finger at a brother and judge him, Love will remind you that he is the Holy Child of God and is crying out for your love and compassion. If fear would drag you into a cesspool of guilt, Love will lift you up into the heaven of innocence and freedom. Let Love be your mentor and guide. Let Love show you that you are ever safe and protected. Let Love reveal to you how valued and cherished you are.

Freedom is your rightful inheritance, and to claim your inheritance all that is required is a simple choice. If it is your desire and your intention to walk upon this planet as an awakened master, make the choice for Love. Set aside time daily to rest in the stillness and abide with me in the peace that lies within. Let this peace dismantle all the obstacles to Love that you built to save yourself from the non-existent demons you have dreamt up. It is not a difficult choice to make. This decision for Love is the only one that will lead you out of a world of chaos into the calm and order of the new world. Will you make this choice now or will you continue to force your will upon a world you cannot save? Only by stepping into the Grace Stream of the Father's Will can you find the happiness you seek. Let go of all striving and let this stream carry you into the depths of peace.

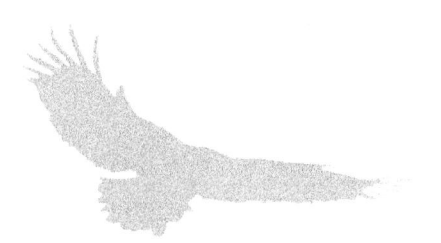

The Voice of Wisdom

Those who choose the path of awakening and remembrance will know the joy to be found in the recognition of the Oneness of God's Creation. Those who open their hearts to Mother Earth will feel their connectedness to the natural world – the rocks that tell of aeons past, the standing trees that grow tall and gracious towards the heavens, the fish that dart about in the cool waters of a mountain stream, the mighty eagle that swoops down to grasp the fish in its talons. All is a beautiful expression of the Love that the Father is.

The ebb and flow of the ocean waves exemplifies the ebb and flow of life. A flower comes into form and then withers and dies. An animal emerges from the birth canal of its mother, travels through its allotted time frame, and is then consumed by a larger beast. A human child begins its life journey as a tiny form, grows into maturity, and when the time is ripe, the consciousness leaves the body, and the material form is returned to the elements. This is the dance of the energies of Creation. Form manifests and then returns to the nothingness. If you can relinquish all attachment to form, all expectation of how things should be, you will experience the wonder and beauty of the manifest world. This divine interplay of energies is an expression of Love. Rejoice that this is so, and free yourself from the limitations of fear and resistance.

Only Love will guide you to appreciation, and appreciation

will bring lightness to your heart and joy to your soul. The way before you need not be fraught with difficulties if you do not resist what is. Allow yourself to trust your Self, your brothers and sisters, and the course of events playing out before you. Have no recourse to denial and defensiveness, because they will but hinder your journey. Ensure that *nothing* is unacceptable to you. Only as you trust and allow everything to be as it is will you begin to see the Love that is the essence of all.

You have convinced yourself that you understand yourself and the brothers and sisters who walk with you in this dream world. You think you know who they are and what they need. You make assumptions about why an event occurs and why symptoms manifest in the body. When you judge a brother if his behaviour appears critical or antagonistic, you fail to recognise his call for love. You believe in the reality of what you see, but you see nothing as it really is. You see only images constructed in the mind to give shape and form and colour to the dancing energies of the One Life. You see only an illusion. And yet because you perceive these images out in the world, you have come to believe they are real. We have told you that only Love is real. This is not a statement made idly. *Only Love is real*. Only Love, the Love that emanates from the Creator, is real, and it is this that shapes your experience.

Love is the essence of all things. Because Love is who you are, you project it outwards into all that you see and experience. We emphasise this now because, if you can come to appreciate how distorted your perception is, you will begin to question your certainties and your judgements. Only when you do so will you begin to experience the Truth shining out from all things. The illusion must be questioned if you would be set free. Freedom lies not in seeing as the small self sees, but in seeing as the Father sees, and He sees only Love.

Put aside *all* judgement and acknowledge that you do not know

Chapter 3: The Voice of Wisdom

what anything truly is nor what it is for. Only as you go within and listen to the voice of the Comforter will you learn of the truth that you seek. As the forces of change unleash their power upon the planet, it is the voice of wisdom, the guidance of the Holy Spirit, that will guide you through any confusion. It is pointless to think that you can do this alone. Indeed, you are never alone, and you are never separate from your Creator. If you are fearful, where will you find reassurance? If you feel lost and insecure, where will you find sanctuary? Who will you turn to for solace and guidance? Only the voice of the Holy Spirit will remain calm within you, guiding your every step, reminding you of the Truth.

Do not doubt that the Earth is moving into a new paradigm. Changes are necessary to cast off the old insane matrix that has crippled the planet and held mankind in a prison of suffering and limitation. Mother Earth is calling out to you to follow her through the metamorphosis. Will you trust that from the ashes of the old world a new world will rise? If you see the downfall of old institutions, do not grieve. In their place will appear structures based on fellowship and cooperation. Honesty, openness and integrity will be the values that guide relationships. This will be the heritage of those who are willing to abandon fear, trust in the events unfolding and acknowledge the Reality of Love.

Beloved friends, we say to you again – you are not alone and have never been alone. All is well. You remain as you were created to be. Because this world is but a dream, you are always safe and *will* awaken to that which is real. Scenes of discord and disharmony remain as images in the mind. They have no reality. But you can choose instead to step into a happy dream, a dream where defensiveness and attack have no place. This is your choice.

The 'happy dream' is an analogy. When you 'wake up' from the old way of thinking and being, your mind will no longer be clouded by false concepts that steal away your peace and equanimity. This world as you see it remains an illusion, a fabrication of mind. It appears as a collection of images in the mind that you have thought up. When you initially relinquish fear, what you will experience is the happy dream. This world is imagined, but when based on thoughts of Love, it will appear as a harmonious world, a beautiful world rich in joy and abundance.

It is when you fully wake up to the realisation that it is but a dream that you are set free. You continue to dream but you know you are dreaming. You can be in the world but not of it. You will no longer become lost in drama or confusion. You will see the face of God in everyone you meet. Such is the joy and power of awakening.

All that you experience now is what you have chosen. You are not a victim of anything outside yourself. Indeed, there is nothing outside of your Self. You experience what you have decided to experience. When you look upon disaster, it is because you have chosen to see disaster. When you perceive suffering, it is because you have chosen to perceive suffering. When you want only Love, you will see only Love. You are not small, and you are not limited. You are Christ and the Power of God lies within you.

It is important that you become fully aware of how powerful you are. The small self sees itself as restricted, as insignificant, as weak. It sees itself as a body, contained within the boundaries established by the body. It believes that it can suffer pain and that it will die. But you are not the body. The body is but an implement, a device that can be used as an instrument of communication, an instrument of Love, a device that can be a means of bringing peace to this planet. Honour it for the role that it fulfils. Cleanse and care for it and meet its needs for nourishment and shelter – but do not give it a power it does not possess.

It is the I AM in you that is your strength and your way-shower. All power under Heaven and Earth is yours because it is the Father who does all things through you. It is not the body or the small self

Chapter 3: The Voice of Wisdom

that does this. This is the illusion that has held you bound by its lies for too long. It is time to see beyond the illusion, to see clearly that all that you have believed to be true is a distortion of truth. The world you see is not real. What is born in time must surely die – and that which is subject to death has no reality.

When you look upon the world around you, what will you see? Will you choose to see disaster and respond with anxiety? Or will you see beyond the illusion and see Love crafting out a new world? You will not experience inner quietness until you acknowledge the unreality of the dream. Because your soul is crying out for peace, for a release from apprehension and suffering, you can choose to respond to the cries of your soul and heed the wisdom of the Heart. For the Heart knows only of Love. The Heart whispers of the beauty and harmony that is to come. The Heart bids you to trust and allow because it knows that all is well, and there is nothing – *nothing* – to fear.

Fear feeds upon itself. Fear builds on fear until the small self becomes lost in the nightmare of its own creations. The ego will seek confirmation of the rightness of its reactions and grasp onto the perceptions of others who are driven by fear. Fear can become as a cancerous growth, spreading its toxicity deeper into your awareness. The ego, reluctant to accept responsibility for its emotions, will seek to justify its fears, projecting blame onto the world that seems to be outside itself. It will vehemently defend its opinions and resist the wisdom that calls for trust and acceptance for what is. When it builds these walls against the Truth, trepidation and unhappiness will increase.

Fear, by its very nature, carries with it the burdens of tension and disharmony. You cannot know peace while you are held captive by the bonds of fear. Love, however, is gentle. Love is kind. Love embraces all that you are and all that your brother is, without judgement. Love is unconditional. Love does not find fault but sees the truth that God's creations emanate. It honours your journey and grants you free will to do what you have chosen to do. It does not attack or defend. It allows all things and trusts all things. It sees the Light of Christ radiating from all God's children, and thus it sets them free. The option to choose Love or fear has been granted freely to you. Which will you choose? Which will you live?

Beloved friends, heed my words, for I come before you now as one who loves you. I come before you to honour you and cherish you, not as someone above me or below me, but as my very Self. We are always One, reflections of each other, reflections that have been projected out into the world in the form of a body and a personality. But this form is not who you are. You are so much greater than this. Let this knowing rest in your consciousness now and be uplifted by the awareness of God appearing as you. Your very essence is divine and shines forth unhindered by any obstacles of thought or feeling. You are free. You are infinitely precious. You are the light of the world, and no one, and no thing, has the power to dim that light.

The Pillar of Trust

Trust is the central pillar that upholds the temple of the Living Christ. It is the light that shines brightly from the eyes of the awakened child of God. The trustful demonstrate a confident bearing and an honesty of speech. They allow and embrace all things and know that there is nothing that needs to be changed. Beloved children of God, trust fully in all that you experience and know that everything that occurs is in your best interests.

Remember that all is well. *All* is well. These are not words we use lightly to comfort you and ease your concerns. We speak but the truth. All is well, now and always. Look about you now, and trust all that you see. Trust your Self. Trust your God. Trust the universe and all it presents to you. There is nothing wrong. There are no accidents. Not one thing is out of place.

In the great orchestration of this dream world, it seems that much suffering is occurring, and you grieve for the pain that others experience. But please remember, it is only that – experience – experience that is freely chosen. Let those who have elected to experience famine do so. Let those who walk through a burnt-out city in anguish do so. Let those who have elected to watch their loved ones killed do so. *It is their choice.* Never are you forced into anything. You have drawn to you every item, every event that you meet. Accept this and be at peace.

The pathway leading you home is laid out by your Creator. Be assured that this is so, and trust in this. As you travel along this path, embracing the Truth of who you are, the radiance of Christ will shine through you. You will want for nothing. Your needs will be met, because the Holy Father provides all that is necessary for His children to fulfil the roles that He has established. Therefore, take no heed of what tomorrow will bring but live fully in this moment now. Be totally present in the environment in which you find yourself.

When you meet a brother or sister along the road, remember who they are. Trust in who they are, because they are Christ manifesting in form. And when you greet them, remember the encounter is sacred, because they are the expression of the Love that is emanating from the One God. What you see in them is but the mirror image of yourself. If you see ought that you would judge, you have only judged yourself. That which you would ask of him, ask it of your Self. For what answer could he give you that would reveal Truth more clearly than the answer your Self could give you? The wisdom that lies within you is all that you need to advise you and guide you on your journey.

Rest often in silence and listen to the still small voice of the Comforter. Learn to have faith in this voice. Trust that you are deeply loved and are being guided in each moment. Because you do not know what the world is and what it is for, the Holy Spirit will guide you. It will direct you gently into the quiet places of peace. It will lead you to those people in need of counsel, those calling for one who knows the truth. When you can open your mind and your heart and can learn to trust what *is*, fear will find no place to cling to in your consciousness. Fear can only gain a foothold in a mind that has abandoned trust.

What do we mean when we suggest that you do not know what the world is or is for? Indeed, you do not know, because how can the small self realise and contemplate the true majesty and magnificence of the Father's Creation? This is not possible. Because the small self, so blinded by fears and judgements, does not see clearly. It sees only its own projections, pictured beyond itself so that it will not be obliged to take responsibility for its experience.

The small self is insane, and the insane see an illusory world distorted by false perceptions and fear-driven emotions. Be assured that we do not judge you or deride you for this blindness. We love you dearly, but you are lost in a dream that you believe is true. The dream with all its dramas and distortions seems real to you but it is but a dream. But while you yet cling to the beliefs you hold, you will not escape the nightmare.

You believe that you are small and limited. You believe that you are a body which can become ill, get hurt and die. You believe your brothers and sisters are separate from you and are worthy of your judgement. You have forgotten your Self, forgotten that there is nothing outside of you. When you rest upon your bed, you think the bed is supporting you. When you don your garments, you think that the body needs to be clothed. When you drive your car, you believe that you have travelled from one place to another. None of this is true.

You are pure spirit, pure conscious awareness. You are no thing, nothing, but because you are consciousness itself, you have the power to dream of worlds and universes without end. We call on you now to awaken from the dream and embrace the Truth of who you are. No, you do not know what a single thing is or is for, because only Love is real. You think the pillow on your bed is to cushion your head, but it is Love that you have projected on the screen of your mind. As Love, its purpose is to shine forth the Love of the Father in all its glory. You think the food that you eat is absorbed by the body to nourish and sustain its cells. But this food is the expression of Love in form, and its purpose is to shine forth the Love that the Father is.

All is indeed well in the world. Trust in *all* that is unfolding, in your life and in the broader events occurring in the world. Let each soul experience what they have chosen to experience and celebrate their divinity as they do so. It matters not what unfolds in the lives of those walking through the dream, for dreams are fleeting, as whisps of clouds that float away to nothing. But your reality as Christ is unchanging forever. Your light never dims.

Be assured that only Love is real but realise that the Love of the Father is beyond the conception of the mind. As the new age dawns, the world will awaken from its confusion and disharmony. It will come to know the Peace of God and treasure the Love that rests in the heart of all things. I ask you now to trust, trust in the unfolding of events. Trust that you are the holy Child of God and are awakening into the realisation that you are eternal and unlimited.

To trust is not to hope. Hope is wishful and anticipates a change in circumstances. Trust however is sure. The one who trusts is the one who is certain, one who looks out upon the world and allows all to be just as it is because that one knows that *all* is well. The one who trusts does not hesitate but acts with conviction and confidence and speaks with calm authority.

Beloved friends, trust in what you are feeling. Know that emotions do not need to be feared. Do not judge yourself when you experience sadness or anger or despair. They are neither good nor bad, neither right nor wrong. They simply are. Trust *whatever* you experience. Allow the emotions to flow and feel them as they arise. If you are feeling angry, simply allow the emotion to arise and move through you. Do not judge yourself for what you feel. The habit of suppressing emotions is an ancient one, because in your innocence you judged them as inappropriate, unspiritual or even perilous. Simply trust all emotions and allow them to arise without resistance.

What can you do when your trust is weak, and fear takes a hold in your mind and shatters the peace of the body? You have only to stop, rest in the quietness and bring your attention to your breath. Let each breath deepen and move with intention through the tension that the anxiety has brought forth. As you breathe deeply into the belly, begin to sense the stillness and silence that awaits you beyond the talons of fear. With each slow breath, sense the Truth that lies in this tranquil place within you. Abide here silently and feel the presence of the Father, the One God. The strength of this Presence will gently remind you that all is well, and fear has no reality. Feel trust begin to grow, bringing serenity and reassurance. Remember that only Love is real and all the problems that loomed so large are but distortions of truth, coming to reveal to you those aspects of your awareness still lost in the illusion.

When you come to realise that separation is a delusion, when you *know* there is only One, you will be willing to relinquish all illusion of control to that One. You have believed that you are a body and that you are the director of your life. You have relied on the five senses of the body to reveal the world to you, but you have failed to see beyond the veils of fear that have obscured your vision. Old beliefs in scarcity, limitation and fear of the unknown have restricted you. As you learn to trust in what *is*, to trust that the Father's Will for you is perfect happiness, you will begin to see a different world, one that is illuminated by the Light of Love. Trust, then, in who you are. Trust in the Love that birthed you. Trust that the Father's plan for you will lead you home. Trust that there is nothing to fear because fear has no reality.

When you have faith in the unfolding of events, knowing all your needs will be met, you will become as the wind. You will be moved by the Will of God, carried gently from one place to another without concern for your safety or your well-being. It will not matter where you rest your body at night, or from whence the food to nourish you will come, because you will know, if you trust in your Father's plan and willingly act as His instrument, your happiness and your peace of mind are assured. Beloved friends, the blessings of trust are yours for the asking. Choose now to give up all concerns for where you will go and what you will do. Know that you are not living your life – you are being lived. No longer let the small self obstruct the joys of fulfilment that will flow to you when you give up all attempts to direct the course of your life.

If the body becomes ill, do you respond to it with Love or react with fear? If all events are neutral, are you willing to trust what is occurring? Or do you judge the body and berate it? Do you permit the illness to lower your spirits? Do you let fear motivate your actions and endeavour to overcome the symptoms using magical means? Remember that you do not know what a single thing is for. Be assured that all things are done *for* you and not *to* you. The body is not your enemy. Could you place trust in the inherent wisdom of the body and realise that you do not understand why the illness has manifested?

The egoic mind will be quick to respond in its endeavour to convince you that it has the answers you seek. It will provide 'logical' explanations that may bewitch you into believing that it is acting in your best interests. It may try to persuade you that the illness resulted from the food you have eaten, or your exposure to a virus, or a weakened immune system. It matters not what justification it offers. The truth is that you do not know what this illness is or what purpose it holds.

What message is the body offering you? This illness, this affliction, is a gift. It only needs to be accepted and embraced. Therefore, be at peace and allow the symptoms to be expressed without judging them or condemning them. Trust in the intelligence that is resident in the body, and allow, allow, allow. The voice of the Holy Spirit will guide you if you need to take some action.

The way before you will not be marred by difficulties unless you choose to see difficulties. The way before you will be simple and clear if you trust what is manifesting in your world. Trust is the key that will open the door to your freedom. Trust annuls guilt over the past and all worry about the future. It gives rise to a willingness to simply be, here and now. In trust lies acceptance. In trust lies tolerance for the fears of others. Be strong in your trust in your Father's Love and know that all is well.

Those lost in fear may try to persuade you of the validity of their perceptions and attempt to justify their anxieties. Do not be distracted by this but remain quietly confident in the reality of the Love that is guiding the course of events. Do not seek to deny their fears or attempt to negate their concerns. Their apprehension is simply a call for Love. They have forgotten who they really are. Respond with compassion but offer no advice unless it is requested. Open your heart to them and trust in the guidance of the Holy Spirit. Trust in your Self. Your strength can inspire strength and confidence in them and challenge their fears.

In these changing times that the Earth is witnessing, those who trust will thrive. Mother Earth is awakening into a world where Love is the guiding force. The strong will stand as a stronghold of power and wisdom. The trusting will demonstrate that the only clear path to follow is the path of allowance and surrender. Beloved children of God, choose wisely now. Remember that only Love is real, and what is real can *never* be imperilled. Walk with me into the new world now, knowing that all is well and you remain as the Light you were created to be.

The Call for Love

Because there is only One, because separation is a lie, there is no one outside of you. When you look upon a brother or sister, you do but see yourself. It is all your projection. When a brother is crying out for love, how do you respond? Will you recognise that he is part of your Self and respond with love? For he is yourself mirrored back to you. He is the essence of Love. He is Christ. He is the joy of the world, and he is its Light.

When others are trapped in a prison created by their own thoughts, their calls for Love may manifest as anxiety, defensiveness, or aggression. Your task is to see beyond their defences and their manipulations and to know that they stand before you as God in form. If you react with fear, you merely reinforce their beliefs in their own vulnerability.

Whenever another is not expressing love, whenever a fear has taken hold in their consciousness, know that the power of your love can soothe and heal their troubled spirits. Your role is to be the presence of Love that you are. Set no agendas to fix or advise. It is not helpful to believe that you know how others should live their lives. Simply be the Love that you are. The power of your presence has the potential to save many from the deep hollows of despair into which they have fallen. If you think that these words are too strong, that you do not have the ability to help others in this way, I say to you that you are forgetting who you are once again and placing limits on what is unlimited.

We ask only that you be that which you are. To live, to act, to speak as the truth of who you are. To do so you must give up to the tendency to believe you are a body. You must give up thinking that you are small and limited and incapable. You are divine, and your life has the power to heal and mend the minds of men. While I bid you recognise that you are not a body, you are not asked to forget the body. To do so would be madness. You experience being in a body. Do not resist any of that experience. Simply remember that you and your brothers and sisters walk in a dream.

When you are in communion with others, remember who you are. Do not use words carelessly. 'Words may hurt, and words may heal': have you heard these words before? Let your words be healing words. Let them soothe, calm, and caress the weary and the fearful. Let them be a tool to use to respond with love to all calls for love, no matter what form those calls may take.

The call for love is a plea but is not always recognised as such. Look beyond whatever fear, anger or aggressiveness that may arise to see into the heart of the one before you. Know who they are in Truth. Know that they are Christ. Do not fear anything they may say or do. Simply accept all that is occurring in the moment, with love, compassion, and humility. Do not set yourself above them. Realise that they have become temporarily lost in illusion and love them as the Holy Child of God. Your light and your love will do more to heal troubled spirits than all the striving and urgency that rob the soul of peace.

We ask that you be very discerning when another reacts to words or actions they have judged to be threatening. Always do we ask you to speak the truth and to respond to calls for love with love. If you are in a conversation with others who feel that their beliefs are threatened, they may respond defensively. While their opinions are just opinions, idle thoughts in the mind that they are convinced are true, you have only to speak the truth as you believe it to be, while respecting the right of others to express what is true for them.

There are times when it may be appropriate to challenge rigid beliefs and expose them as the illusion that they are. When the words you speak are motivated by Love, they will be heard with less defensiveness and less tendency to react. Speak the truth but remember that, however others respond, it is all your projection. They are yourself mirrored back to you. What you see in them is what you may have failed to recognise in yourself.

Whenever another is calling out for love, in whatever form that manifests, heed that call. Listen to what is being expressed. Truly listen. Do not assume. Do not expect. Listen with an open heart and an open mind. Be aware of what is being said, beyond the words, beyond the cries, beyond the frustration, beyond all the emotions being expressed. Listen and observe. Hear what their heart is calling for. Look beyond the frightened ego, the insistent ego, the angry ego. Look deeply into the eyes of the one before you and know that therein lies the One who is Christ, the One who is God, the One who is Love Itself.

When your heartfelt desire is to respond to all calls for love with love, beware of your own defensiveness. Any disturbance, any sense of unease, your every reaction is a doorway into the depths of your subconscious where fears lie buried. Every time you are disturbed, welcome the reaction as an opportunity to discover what is really unsettling you. Welcome all the unfelt emotions lying beneath the surface of your mind. To respond with love to all calls for love, you must acknowledge your own tendency to react. Be watchful. If someone criticises you, observe your own response with self-honesty. If defensiveness arises, you can choose not to react but go within yourself to discover the underlying emotion that is causing you to feel threatened.

THE ASCENDENCE OF LOVE

Love always speaks the truth. When truth is expressed, it is a blessing and cannot in Reality hurt another soul. However, beware of being agreeable to gain approval. Do not seek to be agreeable as a means of expressing love. It does not. Being agreeable is an action performed to gain love, not to offer it. To join in love at a deep level, you must always be true to who you are. You must be true to all those you encounter and all those you speak of. This is integrity. This is wholeness.

Love is unconditional and holds no expectations of others. Your brothers and sisters do not need your pity or your attempts to save them from themselves. When they are lost in darkness, do not judge them. Do not see them as separate from who you are. If they are calling out for your love and understanding, extend your love to them and honour the choices they have made. Remember that they are your Self reflected back to you. Look upon them and smile because you recognise the great Love that shines from within them. Look gently upon all the suffering in the world and know that you need not be part of the problem but can be part of the solution.

Beloved friends, we love you and are ever One with you. We are not above you or indeed more knowing. We are not above you but because we are not in a body as you know it, we see your world from a different perspective and see the great plays of energy that are moving over the planet at this time. Dramas are being enacted in various parts of your world, but Love has found a foothold in many places where only darkness reigned. Love is seeded in many places because children of light have planted it in ancient seedbeds where it will sprout and grow.

As old fears drop away, Love is growing in hearts and minds throughout your world. Rejoice that this is so, and do not be disheartened by what you see on your television screens. Remember Love always, and its great power to heal and nurture. Love will triumph because there is no greater power than the power of Love.

Even in the chaos observed on the Earth now, Love is alive and initiating its children and revealing the power of its presence to them by exposing the strength and wisdom they hold within themselves.

The Reality of who you are is unchangeable forever. The Reality of who your brothers and sisters are is unchangeable forever. Look upon all that you see with trust, gentleness, and playfulness. It is all Oneness waking up to Itself. Do not take your life seriously. It is not your job to save the world. It is not your job to save your brothers and sisters. Simply be that which you are, and you are the presence of Love. Walk with me now and let us love the world together. Let us bring light and our peaceful presence to all who come before us.

Restoration of Vision

Man has been both saint and sinner. He has loved and he has hated. He has made peace and fought the ugliest of wars. He has sought solace in the deep quiet of the forests and thrived in the haste and confusion of crowded cities. He has known compassion and felt the barbs of scorn. He has reached heights of ecstasy and plummeted into the depths of despair. All this he has done, and more. But when will he cry out 'enough'? When will he realise that only peace will satisfy the yearnings of his soul?

Peace lies always in the depths of your being, waiting for you to be still and silent so that it might gently rise into your consciousness. Only peace will bring rest to minds long lost in the darkness of illusion. Only peace can heal wounds carved deeply into the psyche of one who has known the pain and madness of separation. Choose peace now. In truth it is a choice-less choice because who in their right mind would choose to remain in darkness when the Light of their Father's Love is beckoning them home?

Beloved children of God, will you make the decision for peace and walk beside me now into the loving arms of He who has given us life? Will you take up your cross and follow me out of the shadows of fear into the radiant light of the Father's Love? When I bid you to take up your cross, what do I mean? In Christian mythology the cross appears as a symbol of suffering, a representation of the crucifixion. But I say to you, suffering is never possible. The Truth of who you are is eternal, unlimited and free. You are pure spirit, the expression of the Father's Love in form. You are not the body, so do not believe the myths promoted by those who deny their Reality as Christ.

If the cross does not signify suffering, what does it mean? What I accomplished on the cross is the demonstration that life is eternal, and death is not real. I came to show you that *you* are an eternal being and cannot die. Think not that the cross is a symbol of suffering but rather a symbol of the triumph of the spirit which overcomes the death of the body. Think of the cross as a symbol of the resurrection and the power of Love to rise above the dramas of this world. When I bid you to take up your cross and follow me, I do so to ask you to remember your eternal nature and your power to rise above the turmoil of the dream world.

Just as I carried the cross through the streets of old Jerusalem to Golgotha, you too have the strength to face the challenges of this world and walk onwards and upwards to the realisation of truth. You are not small or weak. You are great. You are Love itself, in all its beauty and strength. Rise up off your knees and carry what seem to be your burdens lightly, knowing who you are in truth. Celebrate the cross for what it is: a symbol of the realisation of Oneness, of the triumph of the spirit to rise above the delusions of the ego.

The ways of the world are not the ways of the Father. The world is fraught with self-induced dramas and discord. Brother is at odds with brother. Such is his conviction in the rightness of his beliefs that a brother will maim and kill to force his beliefs upon others. Fear is the motivator, and all thought of brotherly love is lost. Does this bring joy or peace to the one who is so convinced that he is right? Indeed not. His sense of justification becomes as a heavy weight upon his consciousness. This gives rise to unconscious guilt which is then projected outwards.

Chapter 6: Restoration of Vision

Because he so vehemently clings to his conviction that he is right and his actions justified, he willingly sacrifices all happiness to maintain a false and precarious position. Such is the power of the ego that it distorts the truth and disguises fear in the garb of self-glorification. Now is the time to confront the lies and distortions of the ego within yourself. Come to realise that what you long for is not the false and lonely position of righteous grandiosity. It is only the pretentious ego that needs to be seen as 'better than' because it is afraid the world will perceive how small and defenceless it really feels.

When you are being distracted by an electronic device or by the busyness of your life, you are being taken away from your Self. You cannot know who you truly are if your consciousness is diverted away from the essence of your being. Beloved friends, think carefully upon this because you have been deafened and blinded by the array of sounds and images you have thought up to avoid your Self.

Beloved children of God, what you crave is peace. What you long for is quietness of the soul. All the loud and noisy distractions you have manifested in this world are simply that - distractions. You convince yourself you are being informed and entertained but look honestly at what you are doing. Do these distractions bring you heartfelt joy? Do they enlighten you? Do they bring you greater clarity about the illusory nature of egoic perceptions? Do they bring forth deep love in your heart for your brothers and sisters? Do they draw you closer to your God? Look at what these experiences are really giving you, and at what you are avoiding.

The ego would have you believe that you are in control and that you can only be safe and content if you are in command. But the small self has never been in control of anything. It is simply the handmaiden of fear. If you could relinquish all attempts to control your world to the Father and give up all distractions and defences against the truth, you will come to know a way of life that is blessed with love and happiness. What this requires is trust and surrender, trust in the Father who birthed you, and a surrendering of all fearful attempts to control the course of events.

All desire to control springs from the belief that you are separate and alone and need protection from forces outside of you. You construct the walls of your homes to protect you from the environment in which you live. While you abide within these walls you hold an illusory sense of privacy. Then you build fences around your homes to further separate you from the world beyond. You create imaginary lines of demarcation between municipal areas and states, all separating one area from another. In truth, all concept of separation is illusory. There is only One. One Life, One Truth, One God. And all are expressions of the Love that the Father is.

Beloved ones, all boundaries, all barriers that would define your individuality, support the false concept of separation and are not helpful. Our task, then, is to break down these barriers, to turn the tables on the old beliefs that keep you separate, limited and alone. You have never been alone and never will be alone. In all the desperate moments in which you felt so isolated and apart from your brothers and sisters, you yet remained at one with all life. You are, even as you read these words, resting in a cradle of Love. You are never alone and never forgotten. We know you and love you. Your cries for help are heard. We watch over you and respond to your calls.

While you yet believe you are a body, the images that arise in your mind would show you one mass of cells and organs set apart from another. You see bodies that differ in size, shape, colour and mannerisms. But I say to you yet again, you are not the body. Seek not to pass by these words quickly but let them remain clearly and keenly in your consciousness. *You are not the body.*

The body remains the province of the ego, and it strives to

Chapter 6: Restoration of Vision

persuade you that the body is real. It is the illusion of separation that gives the ego its seeming power, because in this way it endeavours to justify its false perceptions. Surely if you are a body and separate from your brothers and sisters, then you must need to control your environment and defend yourself from attack? This is the ego's perception.

Mother Earth is no longer willing to tolerate the presence of a community at war with itself. Now you are called upon to open your heart and remove the blinkers from your eyes. No longer can you continue to play out the old familiar games of judgement and blame, games of attack and defence. A 'call to arms' has sounded, a call not for guns and explosives but wisdom, open-heartedness and love. Will you heed this call and place your trust in the events being precipitated?

The egoic mind is a defence against the Truth. It is the bastion of false perceptions behind which you hide and which you trust will protect you from what is 'out there' that you fear and would avoid. But all barriers to Truth must be destroyed. *All.* Because only the Truth will release you from the nightmares within which you have become lost.

Go within and seek out the darkness of the ego. And what does the darkness signify? Merely your failure to embrace the truth of who you are. Because the darkness represents your shunning of those parts of yourself you do not want to acknowledge and embrace. The ego hides from the very qualities from which it could learn, because it fears them. You have feared to look at what you have judged as 'bad' within you, yet all qualities of mankind lie within you – the anger, the jealousy, the resentment, the bitterness, the judgement, the intolerance...

It is time to stop and look into the depths of your awareness to see all that you have not wanted to see in yourself. This does not single you out from your brothers and sisters, because all must come to this point and look within at all they have avoided. Do so not from a place of self-judgement but of childlike curiosity and wonder. As these demons of old enter your awareness, you are not asked to slay them, merely embrace them and love them. Understand that they were born of your belief in separation. They are not evil, only misunderstood. It is time to embrace all you have denied and avoided, because these feelings and emotions are the very obstacles to the awareness of Love's presence within you.

You think you know what the world is and how it functions. You think you know what the things of the world are and what their purpose is. You think that the images in the mind reflect reality. But, as I have often told you, you do not know what a single thing is for. Because how can you see clearly when you see but a projection of your own thoughts and defences? Whatever you look upon, you see but yourself.

Truth is not to be gainsaid. Truth shines out from everyone and everything, but you see it not. All creation is a dance of energies, intricate and beautiful, and radiant with the Father's Love. But you see only what you want to see and not the Love that is the essence of all things. When you want only Love, that is indeed all you will see. Therefore beloveds, it is time to let your vision be restored. It is time to look upon the world, free from the veils created by the ego to hide the Love that is shimmering and shining within all things. If you are willing to make the choice for Love, you will discover that which ends all suffering and turmoil.

The Light of Truth

The way before you is easy. The choice to awaken is the simple decision to elect sanity over insanity. It is the decision to choose Love over fear in every moment. If you make this choice, your experience of the world will be very different. You will come to know a peace in the depths of your being that is beyond the understanding of the egoic mind. You will experience a joy that is beyond the ken of those still lost in the illusion of separation. You will feel a love and compassion for your brothers and sisters that is sweet and profound. You will see the Light of the Father's Love shining forth from all. You will realise the absurdity of all judgement and perceive that the projection of guilt and blame is madness. Laughter will bubble up within you when you discover that you are set free from limitation and the senseless habits of the old paradigm.

The choice is yours. Therefore, I ask you to make this choice now. For what is to be gained by procrastination? Would you willingly linger in a world riddled with strife and crippled by false perceptions of judgement, guilt and blame? Would you willingly choose unhappiness over happiness, or disharmony over harmony? This is the reality of the choice before you. If you choose to remain asleep in the dream of separation, you will continue to reap the fruits you have always reaped. If you choose to awaken from the familiar nightmare, you will reap the bountiful harvest that awakening brings.

Such is your choice. Insanity or sanity? Do not hesitate. Relinquish all traces of the dark dream and come to join me in Heaven. Heaven is not a mythical place. Heaven is here – now – and will appear shining before you when you decide to step beyond the boundaries of the old world and claim your freedom.

Why do I emphasise this so strongly? Because it has been your habit to avoid the decision. The egoic mind has convinced you that you are separate and alone and must control your own life. It has convinced you that hell is Heaven, and Heaven but a dream of the imagination. It has persuaded you that the insanity of the ego is in fact normal and sensible and sane. Your thinking has become so distorted that you have lost sight of what is true and believe your dream is real.

I come to you now to shake the walls of your self-created prison and break down the barriers you have erected to truth. I come to urge you to push open the doors of your cell and step free because you hold the key that will open the door. You will not grow stronger or surer by delaying to make this choice. The Truth of who you are is shining forth as a radiant star upon the world. Will you shake the cobwebs of sleep from your eyes and let yourself see the truth? You are a miracle of creation. You are the expression of God's Love in form, and you are infinitely precious. Open your eyes and your heart and let yourself see the real world shining before you.

Beloved friends, awaken *now* to the truth of who you are. Do not wait for a future time when you believe that conditions might be more favourable. Awaken now to all that you are and all that you can be. While you believe that awakening will occur sometime in the future, so it will be. *This* is the only moment there is. Time is an illusion. Rest quietly now and let the awareness of Reality flood your consciousness. If you believe this is not possible now, you will limit your experience.

Is it possible for you to awaken from the dream now? Indeed, it

Chapter 7: The Light of Truth

is. Wait for the right moment no longer. *This* is the moment to unlock the gates of your prison and step free. When you emerge from sleep after a night's rest, is it something you struggle to do? Indeed not. It seems to just happen, does it not? Awakening from the dream of separation will be just as simple, just as easy. It will seem as though it 'just happened.' But it will happen by your choice. It will happen because you believe it is possible. It will happen because you no longer create obstacles to awakening. Precious friends, will you continue to cling to false beliefs, or will you step free from the prison cell that has kept you captive for far too long?

The ego will endeavour to convince you that you are small and helpless and alone. It will beguile you with its logic and its analysis of the world. But the ego is not wise. It is not knowing. Its mechanisms of control and manipulation are initiated by fear. The essence of your being is Love, and when Love speaks, fear recedes. Wisdom does not reside in the head but in the heart. When you trust in the heart's wisdom, it will lead you away from fear into the light.

The ego is a construction of mind and is revealed by the constant stream of thoughts running through the mind. These thoughts need have no relationship to the present moment. They may arise out of unresolved issues in the past, or concern over what might happen in the future. They might be a reaction to events that have just occurred and carry strong emotional overtones. Thoughts and emotions are intricately linked. Thoughts will give rise to emotions, and emotions will give rise to thoughts. You have come to identify with them, and you think that they have meaning and value. You believe they are an expression of your being, but this is not who you are. You are pure conscious awareness. You are formless, and you are limitless and free.

When you look into a mirror, you see a reflection of what you believe to be you. Depending on your state of mind, you will judge what you see favourably or unfavourably. But what you are seeing is a false image. When you observe the world through the physical eyes, you are looking through the many veils of expectations, old beliefs, denials and suppressed emotions. You are blind to the real world. You are blind to the real you. When you look upon this mirror image, believing it to be you, you see it aging over time, and believe that it will die. Know that what is changeless cannot die. What is timeless is beyond the clutches of time. Trust in the certainty that you are not the body but are infinite and unbounded.

Because you have believed yourself to be a body, you have been concerned about its welfare and appearance and fear its annihilation. You become fearful when it is diseased or injured, believing yourself to be a victim of the condition, forgetting your true nature. If it appears unattractive and unlovable, you judge yourself as unattractive and unlovable. But I say to you again, you are not the body. You remain as you were created to be. Because you are responsible for your experience in this world, you are not a victim at any time. It is impossible for you to be a victim. You have freely chosen the life that you are living. You chose it because you desired it. When you look upon the image in the mirror, do not judge it or berate it. Honour it as the manifestation of Divine Love in form, a vehicle of expression to reveal the reality of Love to all humanity.

The ego claims the right of ownership. It believes it can own what it perceives beyond itself. It declares that this is 'my' spouse, 'my' child or 'my' property. This provides it with the justification it seeks to control a person or a situation, or to exclude others from sharing in the joys of ownership. All concepts of ownership are a delusion and are an obstacle to the realisation of the presence of Love. Observe your behaviours and patterns of speech to determine where you have claimed possession of an object or another person. Relinquish all sense of ownership and rest in the truth that there is only One – One Life, One God, One Truth. You are not separate from your brothers and sisters. You and all that you look upon are a

Chapter 7: The Light of Truth

manifestation of the Father's Love and cannot be owned.

The ego's mechanisms of struggle and suffering give it the illusion of life and meaning. You struggle to achieve happiness. You struggle to be healthy. You struggle to earn a living, and you struggle to survive. You have been persuaded that suffering supports your personal growth and evolution. You believe that the most challenging times in your life have taught you valuable lessons. While you abide on this planet, everything that you experience is of value, but suffering is not necessary. It is born of the belief in separation. In Truth you are not separate from your God and do not need to 'learn' and 'grow'. You are the essence of Love. You are Light. The Truth of your being is changeless and eternal. Let go of all belief in suffering and see the joy and sweetness of the life that lies beyond all your struggles.

Become aware of the ways that you remain entrenched in egoic thinking. Can you embrace your limitless freedom as pure spirit, as pure consciousness, and realise that there is nothing – *nothing* – that you need do? There is nothing that you *should* do. You do not have to suffer. You do not have to love others. You do not have to earn a living. You do not have to survive. When these words echo through your mind, are you aware of resistance arising? You are a free spirit. The power of God resides within you. There are no forces controlling you, dictating how you should think or how you should act. You are the offspring of the One God, made in the image of the Father, and have but to awaken to your reality as Christ.

The ego is governed by rules. It would convince you that you 'should' do this, or 'must not' do that. Your task is to recognise the restrictions that the ego has placed upon you and observe the ways they have limited you. In Reality there are no rigid rules. You *need* do nothing. Look about you and observe your own behaviour and the way you interact with the world. How much of your life is controlled by 'shoulds' and 'musts'? Set yourself free from these old patterns and live your life as a Christ. Does this mean that you will choose not to earn your living? That you will not love your brothers and sisters? That you will not choose to survive? Indeed not. But whatever you decide to do will be done freely, without the fetters of old expectations and beliefs and you will no longer be constrained by need.

The ego is your nemesis. It will attempt to convince you that it is acting in your best interests, and all the while it is keeping you in hell. The media of your world depict the strife prevalent on the planet: the destruction of life and property that is justified in the name of self-defence; the religious organisations which control and manipulate their congregations, using the 'rightness' of their beliefs to vindicate death and torture; the corruption within governments, the police and the military; problems providing clean water and food; the pollution of the air and waterways excused in the name of 'progress'. In many ways the quality of life within the dream appears to be threatened.

There is no 'right' or 'wrong'. No 'good' or 'bad'. All events are neutral. *You* decide what an occurrence, a situation, will mean to you. *You* interpret events and decide how you will react to them. How then will you choose to respond now? Will you remain in the fog of egoic thinking, crippled by insane fears, or will you step into the new paradigm and claim your Christhood? Will you support the creation of the new world?

If all life on planet Earth were to become extinct, the children of God would remain as they were created to be, infinite and eternal. They would continue to create worlds of experience. But if you wish to live at peace in a peaceful world governed by good will and harmony, listen only to the Voice of Wisdom, and let Love be your counsellor and your guide.

The End of Days

In this time of change the thought systems of old will not benefit you. The past tendencies to see yourself as separate from others and the planet, to seek protection for yourself, to judge and blame the external world, these tendencies will no longer serve you. Your world is changing. The vibration of the earth is rising. Egos are making their last desperate attempt to keep control of the minds of mankind.

When you look about you and see the expressions of anger, the wars and rebellions, the wanton destruction of life and property that is present upon Mother Earth, do not grieve or despair. Look upon them with equanimity. All anger needs to be released. When a people have been subjected to control, suppression, intimidation and violence, anger is the natural consequence. If the people are too afraid to give expression to that anger, does it mean that it is annulled? Indeed not. It remains present in the group consciousness of the people until it is released. When people held in long subjection vent their anger and rebel, it is a necessary part of their healing – and so too the healing of the planet.

You are urged to trust all that is occurring within the dream. The dramas and discords demonstrate the great call for Love being sent out to the universe. Do not judge your brothers and sisters who give expression to their ancient pain. Bless them and honour them.

THE ASCENDENCE OF LOVE

They are aspects of the One, aspects of your Self, and are calling out for love. It is not helpful to judge them or be alarmed by the troubles you see occurring around the world. In this dream world, what you see is always an out-picturing of what is held in the mind. I remind you that when you want *only* love, you will see nothing else.

Can you accept the dramas taking place upon the planet without resistance? And can you accept responsibility for what you are seeing? Only Love heals. If you allow all events to take place without judgement, without fear, trusting that what is occurring is in the best interests of all, you will raise your own vibration and support the resurrection of the planet. The new world will be made manifest. The script is written, and the actors in the drama are playing their part. Will you play your part as an awakened Christ, loving what is, knowing nothing is separate from you?

You are now moving into a new stage of awareness, a new stage of being. No longer use the past as an excuse to justify what is occurring in the present moment. The past is dead. It was just a mad dream dreamt up by a fearful ego which sought to be in control of its own experience. Your life, your creativity, your being, this is gifted to you by your Father. You are not, and never have been, in control of your life. This is the illusion that the small self has clung to for eons. But let this delusion impair you no longer. You are free. You are limitless. You are the precious offspring of the God of Love. The illusion of control must be dispensed with now. Cast it aside as a broken toy, useless and unwanted.

How can you claim to have control of your life when you are as a droplet of water in an infinite ocean, swept one way or another by the movement of the whole? There is no separation. You are not an isolated self-contained unit apart from the All. When a wave arises from the surface of the ocean, does it do so as a separate entity apart from the ocean? Indeed not. The ocean sweeps and rolls, surges and falls, moving as a whole according to its own rhythms. You are pure spirit, manifesting as energy, dancing and playing to the tune of a divine orchestra. You are moved by forces beyond your conception, just as the droplets of water in the ocean move, not by their own volition but swept up in the wondrous play of the whole. Your life is stage-managed by divine forces, and no concept, no accomplishment that you experience, is separate from the One. Nothing is outside of God. Not a single action. Not a single thought. All is God.

We have reminded you often that you are responsible for all that you see. And we have also told you that you do not govern your own life. How can this be? Your life is indeed being orchestrated, and there are no accidents in creation. And yet it seems that you have choices to make, does it not? You do have choices to make, and it appears that you, the small self, is making these choices. Your experience in this world is a product of these choices. Thus, you can be said to be responsible for your experience. But stop and look at how these choices are made.

Thoughts, ideas, appear in the mind. From whence do they come? All minds are joined. Everything that you all think, speak or do is as a ripple in a pond, reverberating out into the world. You may overhear a remark in a shopping centre or problems within your community may motivate you to action. A brother may lend you a book or magazine that brings a new concept to your mind. A teacher may express an opinion that offers you a new perspective on an issue. It matters not from where the thought comes, for the One Mind knows no boundaries. You are never separate from the whole, and no decision is made in isolation from the whole.

You have been 'programmed' by your culture and the society in which you live – by your parents and siblings, by your teachers, your friends and the media. Can you perceive the impossibility of making a choice apart from the All? There is only God expressing, and you are a precious and intricate part of that expression. Do not doubt that you are One with all life, and are incapable of making decisions in isolation, apart from God, apart from all that is. And do not doubt that you are responsible for all you experience. Indeed, because you are that One, you are in Truth responsible for the whole world.

Only the ego would shirk this responsibility. To the ego, it seems a great burden because it believes itself to be small and separate from all that is. But you are not the ego. Because you are pure consciousness, there are no boundaries to your being. Because you are the offspring of a loving God and not separate from your Source, your strength and your power comes to you from your Father. You have no life outside of God. When you relinquish all concept of a separate self who needs to be in control its own experience, you will realise that it is the Father who lives through you. When you give up trying to direct the course of your life and let the Will of God be expressed through you, you will discover a peace and joy beyond your conception. 'Not my will, but Thine be done' – let these words rest in your consciousness. Live them. Why? Because you have realised that of yourself you do nothing, but it is the Father who does all things through you. Herewith lies peace. Herewith lies fulfilment.

Troubled times are evident on the planet now, but you can follow the course of these events without fear, reaction or retaliation. We have stressed that there is nothing wrong because these events are precipitating the emergence of your Earth Mother into a new paradigm. Be guided by the Will of the Father and stand as a sentinel of peace and sanity, demonstrating that all is well in Truth. Seek not to stem the tide of change or attempt to control what will seem to be out of control. All such endeavours will fail in their purpose and serve only to increase fear. You are safe, and there is nothing to fear. You are not a body and death is an illusion. Nothing that is real can be imperilled. Therefore allow and trust what is occurring, and relinquish control into the hands of the Creator.

Chapter 8: The End of Days

The time of the end of days is upon you. When you conceive of this, do you picture a period of great catastrophe and devastation? Do you imagine the world coming to an end and all hell breaking loose upon the earth? But 'the end of days' signifies the end of time itself. Time is an illusion in which you have believed throughout human history, and yet it is not real. Such has been the power of your belief that you have created a whole world of experience around the concept of time. You have created units of measurement to structure your lives – minutes, hours, days, years – and you believe that time extends on a continuum into the future.

The concepts of past and future are a delusion because now is the only 'time' there is. All you ever experience is this moment now. Your thoughts about the days past or the days ahead are merely thoughts in your mind and in truth have no validity. And yet you believe in them so strongly and have convinced yourself that they have power over you. You worry about what has been, and experience guilt and self-judgement over some act you committed that is now just a memory and has no reality. The past is past. It is dead. Do you not have a saying 'Let the dead bury the dead'? So let go of the past, bury it deep, and do not allow it to disturb your peace or carry you away from your experience of what is occurring *now*. This moment is precious. It is alive with joy and the riches of life and love and beauty. Why would you cling to the dead when life is calling you forth to love and appreciate what is before you right now?

You make assumptions about what you believe will happen in the future, but they are only assumptions. This 'future' that you have created in your mind is not real, and every precious moment that you spend in this imagined place is robbing you of the full experience of this moment now. You worry about what may happen because you fear life. You are comfortable in the predictability of your days because you believe that you can safely anticipate what will happen.

Your desire for safety and security limits you, and so you rescind the wonder and joy of spontaneity.

You choose to go to the same job each day, travel the same route, follow the same routines, because you believe you can safely foresee what is going to occur. In truth you do not know what will happen in the next moment. You feel secure in what seems unchangeable, but because it keeps you on the same customary pathways you have long walked, you do not walk freely, spontaneously or without inhibitions. An abused wife will stay in a violent relationship because it is what she has been accustomed to, choosing the familiar pain to the uncertainty of the unknown. A man will stay in the same dissatisfying job for many years because it provides him with the security of an income, and he is too fearful to leave and explore other possible ventures.

All worry results from the belief in separation and the lack of trust in what is. It causes tension in the body and can lead it into ill health. It is a form of fear that is crippling. Set yourself free from this insane belief in an illusory future. Take a leap of faith into the fullness of life. There is nothing to fear. When you give up all concept of personal will and allow the Holy Spirit to guide you, all your needs will be met. It is indeed a wondrous and benevolent universe when you take off the blinkers of fear and free-fall into God.

We have urged you repeatedly to choose Love over fear, and to choose to abide in this world as Christ. When you realise that there is nothing to fear, your choices will not appear difficult. The era of the end of days is here. The Earth is changing and evolving, and there is nothing you can do that will hinder this transformation. Decide to be that which you are in Truth. In the new world, fear will be no more, and the Light of the Father's Love will shine in all its glory upon the planet. Rejoice that this is so, and step boldly out of the old parameters into the new.

Chapter 8: The End of Days

Beloved friends, you are deeply loved. You are valued and treasured. When you embrace this knowing fully, you will understand that *everything* is working to serve you. Love is what you are and what you share with all your brothers and sisters. It is what binds you together as One. Though the physical eyes might see disparity and discord, there is in Truth a great web of interconnecting energies that link you all in the magnificent tapestry that is Creation.

Love is on the ascendence now, awakening dormant energies, challenging old belief systems, and revealing the insanity of fear. Love is clearing away the debris of ancient ways of thinking and acting, challenging the thought system that advocated judgement and blame and the belief that punishment and defensiveness were justified. Doubt not that, as the old world passes away, Love is awakening in the hearts and minds of mankind.

The Father is infinite and eternal. Love is infinite and eternal. You are infinite and eternal. Abide in the certainty that this is your true nature. Now it is Love that will heal this world. It will restore the wayward to the path of Truth. It will heal the wounds of loneliness and grieving. It will build bridges between those who have been at war with each other. And Love will dismantle the obstacles that have obstructed the road to creativity and fulfilment.

Beloved children of God, I know you. I, who have walked with you through all your experiences of drama and discord, I see who you are. The great mystery of God is alive in you. I know your strength and your commitment, and I know the power of your love. Let us now cut away the last threads of your attachment to suffering. Walk away for the final time from the ill-begotten guilts of the past. Let it all go and know that in Reality only Love remains. Here and now -- Love is. And Love is all there is.

The Reality of Innocence

The parameters are established. A new day is dawning. Love is on the ascendence. The promises of old are being fulfilled. A new world is being born. Old patterns of behaviour are being questioned. Institutions used to establish power over others are failing - not because of anything outside of them but by forces festering within them. The planet is expressing its voice through dramatic climatic changes and geographical upheavals.

No events are to be feared. The neutrality of all events is assured. *You* decide what they will mean to you. You will be the judge of whether an occurrence is pleasing or displeasing, a gift or a cause for fear. Always is this so. So, we speak to you now of the power of your perceptions. In Truth there is nothing outside of you. All people and events that you see as images on the screen of your mind are simply that – images. They seem to dance and play before your eyes, bewitching you with their life and colour, but they remain as images. And why would you fear an image? You can only fear that which appears real to you. Even when a part of your mind would convince you that it is an illusion, yet the seeming reality of this image has the power to elicit a reaction within you.

Fear is a creation of the egoic mind. It is a misperception, a fabrication of mind. It is important that you come to understand the nature of mind and how easily deceived it is by its own creations.

This world you have thought up has no reality, and yet your mind has convinced you that it is real. This is madness and complete self-deception.

Beloved brothers and sisters, heed the voice of the Holy Spirit, for it will remind you of what is real. It will offer you clear vision and lead you faithfully along the path of self-honesty and self-love. It will reveal to you the errors in your perceptions and gently show you what is true. We have told you many times that only Love is real. Only Love loves. Only Love heals. Only Love sees clearly and honestly. Whenever you look out upon your world and perceive discord, go within and ask for the wise counsel of the Comforter. You will be guided to look upon the world with clarity and love, seeing with discernment, without judgement. For the Holy Spirit is that aspect of your mind that is One with the Father. Here peace is to be found. Here healing can be generated. Here Truth shines.

The children of God have been lost in the mire of confused thoughts and images, believing themselves to be victims of painful events. But you are always responsible for your experiences in this world. It is impossible for you to be a victim of anything or anyone. You have set up the pawns on the chessboard of life. You have moved the pieces into position, and all the effects that you experience result from the choices you have made. If you take full responsibility for these choices, you will be able to see the futility of any assertions of victimhood.

The role the victim plays is always a role of weakness. Victims have given away their power and claimed a false position of helplessness and powerlessness. They believe their suffering and impotence are caused by something or someone outside themselves. They adopt the false roles of martyr and scapegoat. But always are you responsible for all that you experience. You are never alone and never without the ability to change your circumstances. You have but to correct your misperceptions and your life will change.

Chapter 9: The Reality of Innocence

If you look back on your life and review all that has happened, the storms you have weathered, the sunsets you have gloried in, the dramas and joys unfolding in a glorious reel of light and movement and colour, can you accept that it is all your own creation? Not one incident has come to you uncalled for. You have ushered them all in to experience it all, to live through it, to learn, to conquer your fears and perceive the ephemeral nature the dream. You experience it, but you are above and beyond it.

The person you dream of is not you, but one you appear to be acting as, temporarily, to taste the joys and the challenges of this life. The past is past, and it is time to see it all through the eyes of the witness, not the participant. You are not the body – you are the observer. You are in Truth not a human being. You are Life itself. You are spirit. You are pure consciousness. And as such you are not a thing, and cannot be slotted into a specific category, boxed within the borders of limitation. You are eternal, limitless and free. You are divine.

It is important now that you begin to understand the attraction that victimhood holds for you. Come to appreciate the ways that victimhood entices you into the mire of its false beliefs. And why is it that you are so readily tempted to play the victim role? What is it that you gain by protesting your helplessness and your powerlessness? Why are you so willing to let the egoic mind deceive you?

Victimhood carries with it the hope of sympathy. After all, if you have been victimised, should not the world feel compassion for your suffering? And if others see that you are suffering, will they not come to your rescue and accept some responsibility for your dilemma? Victims indulge in helplessness and defencelessness in anticipation of rescue and consolation. Thus does the drama of victim and rescuer play out. The actions of the rescuer are the linchpin that holds the whole charade in place. In truth, this is not helpful. The actions of the rescuer merely reinforce the victim's belief in their own weakness and helplessness. It is more helpful to stand back and let the 'victim' learn to discover their own strength.

If you perceive another appearing to be victimised, remember that you do not know what is truly happening or why. Observe your own behaviour and question your motivations, while remembering that all you see is what you have projected outwards. Do you feel tempted to play the rescuer? Do you feel a need to be needed? Do you fear the outcome if you do not save the other from this situation? Do you need to be in control of events? Do you desire to be seen as kind and helpful, someone special? Only Love heals, but how can you know how Love would respond in this situation? Go within and ask for guidance. If action is required, you will be directed as what to say and what to do.

Victimhood is used as a means of avoiding – avoiding unwelcome associations and avoiding unwelcome tasks. If you are weak and helpless, how can you take on obligations that require strength and capability? Avoidance strategies may take many forms: a child developing a stomach ache to avoid school, a sister evincing a painful headache that causes her to miss an important meeting, a brother overwhelmed with work commitments that preclude him from spending time with his family. You need to understand that there are no accidents. Your thoughts create your experience, and every situation you encounter is chosen, consciously or unconsciously.

You are deceiving yourself if you believe that you can be injured, exploited, persecuted or oppressed by another. It is only by your own choice that you can claim victimhood. This self-deception is a denial of your power and capability. It is a denial of your responsibility as the creator of your own experience. And it is a denial of your reality as Christ. In Truth you can never be victimised. You are Christ Incarnate, and the Power of God lies within you.

Victimhood can be the bludgeon you wield to assign blame and punish another. If you believe that others are responsible for your suffering, you will play the victim to induce guilt within them and so cause them to suffer. If you believe that a sister has offended you, you will be convinced that you have been hurt by her and so feel justified in retaliating. Even a simple difference of opinion can cause the egoic mind to feel victimised. Such is the insane perception that governs its behaviour.

The belief in victimhood is a self-deception because it is in truth a mechanism of control. This is contrary to your concept of victimhood as caused by something or someone outside of you and over which you have no control. When a brother adopts the role of victim, does he not do so because he believes it will bring him what he wants? If he wants sympathy, if he wants to make another feel guilty, if he wants to evade a responsibility or avert an action by another, he chooses victimhood as a means to achieve his ends. Whenever fear arises and you react defensively, *you* are choosing to be the victim and believe your reaction is warranted. Only victims feel a need for defence, and only victims attack. You believe that attack is a justified response to a perceived threat, but attack is never justified.

The Son of God is never threatened. His reality as Christ assures his safety and security. Fear is an illusion, an aspect of the dream playing on the screen of a mind that believes itself separate from the Father. The belief in separation is the greatest self-deception. It is this belief that is the foundation on which so many other false beliefs rest: the belief that there is something outside of God, the belief that you are a body, the belief that fear is real, and that judgement and attack are justified. All old beliefs, all perceived needs, all old resistances, must be relinquished if God's children are to embrace their reality as Christ, the Holy Child of God. When you realise your oneness with all that is and understand the absurdity of the belief in separation, all other false beliefs will topple and disappear.

God is, and you are not separate from the Father. As you look about you, feel the presence of the Father reflected back to you from all that you see. God is. All is God, and all is good and holy and beautiful. Let this thought remain in your consciousness – God is. Rest in this knowing, because only an awareness of the presence of God can bring you the deep rest, the deep peace, that you crave. Simply – *God is*. Let these words bring comfort to your soul. Thus, there is no great wisdom to espouse; no elaborate theories to analyse; no agendas to follow. Simply – God is. Abide in this Truth often. Let it be the anthem playing in your mind. Whisper these words in quiet moments and sing them joyously in celebration of Oneness. God is, and that is all that needs to be said.

Transcendence

My beloved friends, many times have I called on you to let go of the illusory fears that have beset you. Many times have I called on you to remember the Truth and to step up as the Christ that you are. Now is the time to transcend the fears and defences of the ego and embrace the Truth of who you are. No longer give credence to the thoughts that have confused the mind and led you away from peace. If the problems of your world seem overwhelming, you will be tempted to believe that you must struggle against the odds to overcome them. But there are not *many* problems – there is only one. That problem is your belief in separation.

When you feel overcome by the discord in the world, when the future looks dark and filled with foreboding, then remember the Truth of who you are. Stop. Stop, and step away from the false beliefs that have limited you and the dark images that you have decreed are real. Stop, and come home to your Self. Come home to what is Real. Let not the shadows of illusion confuse you. Let all things that you see be as they are. Remember that this world that you have dreamt up remains a construct of the imagination, an illusion of thought, and in Reality cannot harm you in any way. The Truth of who you are is not threatened by false fears or misconstrued ideas. You remain as the divine being that you have always been. You are pure spirit, and you are without boundaries, free and eternal and deeply loved.

THE ASCENDENCE OF LOVE

No one nor anything can harm you, nor destroy what has been created in Love by the Father. Thus, enlightenment is not some great transformation that you must seek and strive for. It is not some elusive goal that forever remains out of reach. You are enlightened now, and you have only to recognise this. Perhaps there is nothing I can say that will convince you of the simplicity of this truth. You must discover this for yourself. Hear me again: *you are enlightened now!* You do not need to labour to read and interpret ancient spiritual manuscripts. You do not have to sit in the presence of enlightened masters. You do not have to attain great mystical insights into the nature of reality. You need *do* nothing. You have only to transcend the illusory thought system of the ego and realise the Truth that you and the Father are One, have always been One and will always be One.

When you realise the illusory nature of your world and accept your reality as Christ, you will recognise the futility of all struggles, the falsity of all fears, and the great joy to be discovered by discerning the great light that shines from within you. Many times have we spoken of the absurdity of your fears. Many times have we declared that all forms of judgement and blame are false interpretations of the children of God who walk this planet. How can we convince you that the great light that shines from within you is the Truth of who you are? Never have you been small or insignificant or unloved. Ever do you shine with the brilliant light of the Father's Love. Ever are you safe and loved. When you come to realise this and accept it as the undeniable truth of your being, you are set free to act as the instrument of the Divine, to serve the atonement, and to shine your light upon this troubled world that is crying out for love.

Again and again, we have given you this message. It is not a difficult concept to grasp. You need no academic degrees to understand this. You need not experience some great spiritual awakening to drag from your eyes the veils of illusion. You have

Chapter 10: Transcendence

only to hear what is spoken and recognise that Truth that has been shared with you. You are Christ! You are Love! And you are ever one with the Father. Accept that the separation never occurred. Accept that there is nothing to fear and nothing for which to strive. Accept that the great mystery that is God is shining within you now and is your very nature.

Your essence is Love. What is eternal and changeless cannot be altered by illusions. You endure for eternity, unchanging, unlimited and free. This is the truth of who you are. No one can rob you of the Light that is the core of your being. Beloved children of God, turn away from the darkness to the Light. Turn away from all belief in limitation, fear and conflict. Turn away from any concept that does not embrace the Truth of your Reality as Christ. Turn towards joy and fulfilment. Turn towards Love and the truth of your enlightenment.

Rest in the certainty that you are free and holy and beautiful and have a role to play in the days ahead. You are called on to fulfil that role and lift the burden of fear from the weary souls that have carried this burden for too long. These souls thirst for the living waters of Divine Truth and the comfort of rest in the arms of those who know the certainty of peace. Look about you now and know there is no more preferable time in which you can shine your light upon those walking in darkness. Know that there is no better place from which you can step forward as the Light and Love that you are. Know that there is no greater fulfilment than to offer your love to this troubled world which is desperately seeking rest and nurturance.

Too long has this world been darkened by minds lost in confusion and crippled by false beliefs. It is time to say farewell to the darkness and let Love illuminate the dark corners of the Earth where shadows linger. We cannot give you a magic formula to shift your awareness away from the dramas and discord of this world, but you do not need a magic formula. You need only acknowledge the Truth of your being and let go all beliefs in the idea that you are alone and vulnerable. You need only accept the Truth of your Oneness with the Father and realise that the whole discordant thought system that has corrupted the mind is false. Only Love works because only Love is real. Let love and laughter light up your life and acknowledge the innocence and purity of your soul.

Because you have believed that enlightenment was a goal you could achieve by study and striving, you thought you needed to be more spiritual or more loving. This elusive goal seemed to lie in the mythical future. "If only I could overcome my fears and insecurities!" "If only I could become purer of heart!" "If only I could achieve the serenity of the spiritual masters!" If only... The goal seemed difficult, if not impossible, to attain in the present moment. Now you must rise above these limited beliefs and accept the Truth of who you are.

You can be nothing other than what you are, and what you are is enough. There is no mysterious secret to awakening you must discover, no deep insight into the dimensions of time and space to realise. Come home to simplicity. Come home to acceptance of what is. Give up trying to get somewhere other than where you are right now. Be at peace with what is. Know you are all you ever can be right now and that all attempts to struggle to attain enlightenment are driven by the wayward ego. The ego can never become enlightened, so it struggles to achieve a goal that forever remains out of reach. Do not let the egoic mind convince you that you are not enough or have not achieved enough. You are more than enough. You are everything.

So, abandon all attempts to change anyone or anything. Rather, accept everyone and everything. Allow, allow, and allow. Master the mind by remembering that it does not hold the answers you seek. You have but to listen to the Heart, and it will speak louder than the confused mind. The Heart does not judge, and it does not compare. It sees no separation between the children of God. The

Chapter 10: Transcendence

unenlightened ego, however, because it believes itself to be separate from all others, is fearful and defensive, and its insecurities cause it to judge and criticise and guard itself against attack. It will perceive hostility where there is none and project blame upon another to avoid responsibility for its own choices. No longer heed the voice of the ego but embrace the certainty that you are enlightened now. Transcend the ancient anxiety that has confused the mind, caused you to resist what is and robbed you of peace.

If, as you lie awake at night, fear arises and dominates your thinking, know that this is an opportunity to practise transcendence. Do not resist the fear. Breathe deeply, quietly, and let it manifest before you in whatever form it adopts. Fully accept the emergence of this old adversary. Realise that it is you who have given it the dreadful emanation it elicits, and you can see through the lie it tells. When fear meets no resistance, it is undone. As you embrace the Truth of who you are, you can rise above the fear and enter the peace and quiet joy that awaits you in the expansiveness of the stillness of that moment.

This goal of transcendence is within your reach now and this is cause for great rejoicing. To transcend your fears, to transcend the thoughts of the busy mind that is continually bewailing its dark stories, to transcend the old tendency to believe that there is something wrong that must be righted – this is indeed cause for celebration. We rejoice with you as you become increasingly free of the old ways of being in this world that has kept you imprisoned in a pattern of reactivity, defensiveness and guilt. As you transcend the ego's thought system, it is as though you were casting off an old costume, tired and out-dated, a costume never to be donned again because you no longer resonate with the vibrations it emanates.

The New Earth may seem to be but a fantasy, an imaginary world where Love is alive and shining. Yet it is not far from you now. It is drawing ever closer. In truth, you are drawing closer to it. As you continue to blossom in the light of Truth, the shadows of illusion are withdrawing. As you transcend the thought system of the old world, it is as though a dark mist that has clouded the mind is beginning to disperse. The mist has had no power to harm you or delay you, and as you walk free of its chill fingers, the splendour of the Truth is seen shining forth in all its glory.

We have reminded you repeatedly to embrace the Truth of who you are, but this has been necessary to cement this concept in your awareness. Because it is *you*, and those who share this journey of transcendence with you, who must take the steps to bring forth the new world. It will be *your* love, *your* wisdom, *your* compassion, that will build this new world. This is not a weighty task, because how can those acts initiated by Love be other than richly rewarding and fulfilling?

The egoic mind is a tenacious instrument. It adheres to what it is convinced that it knows, to its own familiar concepts and opinions. It believes it has the answers and resists ideas that challenge its rigid beliefs. A prisoner who has spent a lifetime isolated in a dark dungeon will be fearful of walking free. The mind shies away from the unfamiliar and the unknown. Your minds have been inveigled by the experiences of the past. You have been ensnared by the sounds and images you have been conditioned to accept as reality, so you have come to believe the illusion is real. How then do you respond when we remind you of the Truth of who you are? Your denial and resistance serve only to rob you of peace. Will you let the mind be master or delegate it to its role as servant?

Know that to think and act as other than the Christ that you are is to live a lie. Decide to come now to the edge of the cliff and choose not to look behind. This decision calls for a dramatic change in the way you are living this life you have declared to be your own. It calls for a recognition of your divinity. It calls for the abandonment of the old ways of interpreting this dream world that has appeared so real to you. Stand now at the edge of the precipice and you will become aware that the rocks are beginning to crumble beneath your feet. Renounce all fear and leap into the unknown, trusting that you will be uplifted by the power and grace of Love. Then let it carry you onwards into the heart of the Kingdom of Heaven.

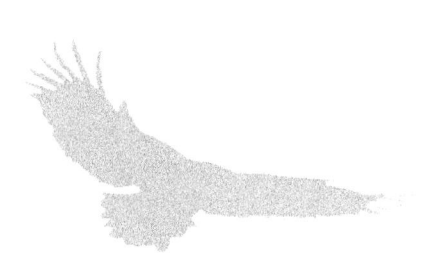

The Nature of Desire

Beloved children of God, it is time to awaken from the dream, and awakening requires that you have a deep longing to live under the auspices of Love. Until this desire becomes a passionate yearning, you will be distracted by the superficial desires of this dream world, blind to that for which your heart sincerely longs.

Until you desire the Kingdom of Heaven above all else, it will continue to elude you. You must want to be the presence of Love in every moment. You must long to rest in the Peace of God, to still the restless mind and sink deeply into the silence beyond all sound. Long to follow the guidance of the gentle voice of the Holy Spirit. Yearn to be all that you are - yearn to be Christ. Until this desire becomes the driving force in your life, you will wander off the path of Truth on useless detours that delay your homecoming and bring you no real peace.

It is easy for you to let the mind be distracted by the amusements you have created to escape being with your Self. You allow your times of peace to be interrupted by what you perceive as obligations, calling you away from the stillness within your Self. You become diverted by electronic devices that fill precious moments with mindless games and images of dramas and discord. In your busyness you evade looking at all the avoidance strategies you use to hide from your Self. Long to know your Self. Long to rest in the quietness of stillness.... because silence is the doorway to peace.

Your thoughts are powerful. If you long for abundance and accept that you are worthy of it, you can manifest abundance, but question why you want it. Do you have a perception of lack or need? When you heed the quiet Voice of the Holy Spirit and want only that which is the Will of God, there will be no compulsion to seek abundance because you will trust that all your needs will be met. You will know that all that is required to serve the Father will be provided.

It is important that you understand the nature of desire. Honestly observe all that you long for. What is it that you really want? To what are you truly committed? How are you filling the hours of your days? Do not read over these words hurriedly. Stop now, sit quietly and dwell on this. What do you really want? Because until the resounding answer is 'the Kingdom of God,' you will still find excuses to avoid, to deny and to procrastinate. Therefore, ask yourself now: 'What do I *truly* want?'

Look well on the events that manifest in your life. Look well on the activities that occupy you in your hours of leisure. What thoughts inhabit your mind? Are you committed to demolishing all the obstacles to the presence of Love? Are you willing to look honestly at your own behaviour and see all the defences the ego has constructed to mask the devious mechanisms it has used to disguise the insanity of its choices?

What you desire is fundamental to awakening. Long to rest in the presence of God always. Long to be who you really are, and to love your God with all your heart and your mind and your soul. Know that this love for your Father is demonstrated by loving your Self. When you judge or berate yourself, you do so by choice. Only the ego judges, because only the ego believes that you are worthy of judgement. Come back to your Self now and observe the choices

Chapter 11: The Nature of Desire

you have made. Be willing to love your Self wholly, knowing that there is only One. When you love your Self, you are extending Love for all the Father's Creation. Therefore, desire to be the Love that you are and extend your love to all.

Desire is the foundation stone of awakening, and all its other building blocks are erected upon it. There can be no commitment without the desire to commit. There can be no allowance without the desire to accept all things as they are. And until allowance is fully embraced, surrender will not be experienced. Desire is the wand you wave to manifest the world you perceive. If you are hungry and desire to eat, you will rise and prepare a meal. If you are tired and desire to sleep, you will move to your place of rest and lie down. Desire prompts the action. Therefore, be mindful of all that you desire. Are your choices leading you forward on the path of Love?

Desire is the threshold from which you step out into the world of activity. It leads you forward on your journey through life. But is it leading you home to your God? Be mindful now of what you want. Be ever conscious that it is your desires that lead you into the next moment. Always are you a free spirit. Always has your Father granted you the power to shape your experience. Willingly desire the Kingdom of Heaven above all things.

With great self-honesty, write down your heartfelt desires. As you rest in the quietness, ponder the question: 'What do I really want?' Do not protest that you do not know. This would simply be avoidance. Be willing to go deeply within, hear your heart's longing and record it. Even if the desire seems impossible to attain or inappropriate, add it to your list. Be utterly honest and do not hide from anything or deny anything. Do not judge what you are writing. Look upon the words on the page with innocence and wonder. Allow all feelings and thoughts to arise unimpeded by fears and insecurities. Do this exercise regularly. After a period of several weeks, observe what you have written. What desires appear consistently in your lists? What do they reveal about what you most value? What prevailing thoughts are being unmasked? Ponder these questions and abide with the truths that are revealed.

In the hours of silence, as the body lies asleep at night, where is your conscious awareness? Do you cease to be conscious? Indeed not. Whether you are driving a vehicle along a busy highway, or travelling through a dreamscape or into other dimensions, you are always aware and always where you desire to be. Even if you are struggling, even if you are suffering, you are experiencing this because you want it. It is impossible for this to be otherwise. You are always responsible for all that occurs to you. This is why it is important that you understand the nature of desire, and that it is desire itself that draws to you all that you experience.

I have told you that it is impossible for you to be a victim. Even if you are in pain and are suffering, you have drawn this situation to yourself. The ego is deceptive and will strive to convince you that you could not possibly desire to suffer. But ask yourself sincerely: 'What do I gain from suffering?' Because no matter what it is that you want, you want it for a reason. That reason that may be conscious or it may be unconscious, but it is a reason you have judged to be valid. Will suffering give you an excuse to avoid an unwelcome event or weighty responsibilities? Will it bring you the love or recognition that you seek? Do you believe that you deserve punishment? Do you think it will teach you compassion? Seek the answer within.

Self-honesty is the tool that will assist you to understand your choices. Clarify in your mind what it is that you really value. Ascertain your priorities. If you really desire to be the presence of Love, would not this be your priority in every moment? If peace is your only goal, why do you manifest situations that create conflict and uncertainty? If you desire the Kingdom of Heaven above all else, why would you choose to react with anger to a brother's remarks,

Chapter 11: The Nature of Desire

rather than see them as a call for Love? Be willing to examine your desires with great honesty, and question what you hope to gain by their fulfilment.

When you are diverted away from the goal of peace, look well upon where your desires are carrying you. When you judge and condemn a brother or sister, you do so because you want to project blame onto them. But each time you do so, you condemn yourself far more harshly. Whether your guilt be conscious or unconscious, you will not escape it. When you desire to be the presence of Love, and extend Love in each moment, guilt will not find a home in your mind.

What you desire is frequently based on what you believe you need. And what you believe you need is based on your perception of who you are. While you believe yourself to be a body and to be separate and alone, you will long for safety and security. You will want approval and acknowledgement. And you will desire material objects that you believe will bring you the happiness that you seek. Thus you struggle and justify manipulation of others to gain what you believe you need.

Beloved friends, want to rest in the silence often, to abide in the quiet places of the Heart where all will be revealed to you. Here you will find the deep peace that is born of trust. Here is the timeless awareness of Love. Here lies the joy that is gifted to those who have razed the obstacles to Love. This silence is the doorway to the recognition that there is nothing that you need do, nothing to seek, nowhere to go, and nothing to understand. Here you can rest in the certainty that you are Christ Incarnate, that you are being breathed and moved by the Love of God. Here you can be certain that of yourself you do nothing, and that it is the Father that does all things through you.

You are never asked to suppress your desires. To do so would be the act of a controlling mind. The suppression of desire leads to a loss of peace. The disciplined mind is the mind that seeks to be in control. If you are fully in allowance of what is, you will not attempt to control your life but simply surrender to the movement of energies in which you abide. To act freely and spontaneously within your world you need not suppress anything. What we advise is that you listen to the desires of the heart and not the head. Be honest with yourself and recognise when you are making a choice governed by a sense of lack or insecurity. Simply question what has prompted your longing.

The time to awaken is now. Do you sincerely desire the Kingdom of God above all things? Do you want it more than the new car or the perfect job? More than that loving relationship? More than great riches? What do your thoughts and actions reveal? You can manifest many things. At no time are you compelled to be loving. You are always free to decide where the next thought, the next moment will lead you. But only the Kingdom of God will bring you the peace that you crave. Only Love will fill the longings of your heart.

Questions are raised about the nature of desire. Some spiritual traditions suggest that desire is worldly and unholy. They equate desire with attachment and dependency. To want is not wrong. To judge any course of action as wrong is a misperception. Desire does not equate with attachment. It is possible to desire something, even as you accept that you might not attain it, or you might lose it once it is achieved. Without desire there would be no creation. Without desire there would be no movement towards awakening. Trust then that desire is fundamental. I ask only that you dwell intently upon what *you* are desiring, on what *you* truly value, and *where* your choices are leading you. Remember the Truth of who you are and no longer be deceived by the false values of this dream world. Follow the promptings of your heart, knowing what it is that you yearn for in the depths of your being.

The Flight of the Eagle

The flight of an eagle, hovering high in the thermals, is uplifting to the soul because it gives rise to the feeling of joy and freedom within us. Elevated at great heights, it floats peacefully far above the events played out on the land below. This regal bird seems to have distanced itself from any intimation of the disharmony and discord that may be taking place on the planet beneath it. And yet the eagle's vision is sharp and reveals the smallest movement occurring below. It nests high in treetops or on cliff tops, in solitary places where it is free and undisturbed. It is a bold and intelligent bird and has become a symbol of strength and freedom.

You can become as powerful and peaceful as the eagle, and be in the world but not of it, elevated above the dramas playing out around you. What would it take? You need not pray more or study more deeply the teachings of the masters. You need not participate in religious gatherings or attend more workshops. No, none of this will serve you. It is all your struggle and your trying that deceives you. Stop trying. Stop seeking. Come home to your Self. Give up looking outside of your Self for answers or fulfilment. You will not find these things by searching for them there. What if you would make this commitment now – to give up the struggle and stop the searching? You have heard me speak of this before, but have you listened? Are you ready to listen now? Or will you read over these words and continue seeking in yet another book or become engrossed in yet another discussion on enlightenment? What will you do?

When I suggest that you stop seeking, I do so because you have become lost in the concepts that you read and hear about. The mind is continually trying to comprehend what it cannot comprehend. And in the confusion that results, you try to grasp for the meaning of it all. You yearn to know, to understand, so again you search for the elusive answers, seeking beyond yourself for what can only be found within. You will not find the Peace of God in the world outside of you. You cannot know Love by searching for it. You cannot know the wondrous joy of an awakened soul while you continue to hold expectations of the world you see outside of you and deny your responsibility for your life and emotions.

Hear me well. Seek no longer for what is already within you. Give up struggling to attain knowledge. Cease the confused mental dialogue that you have believed will resolve your uncertainties. The thoughts of the mind will lead you nowhere, for there is nowhere to go and nothing you need understand. God Is. You are the Holy Child of God, made in His image. And what does this mean? It means that you are not the body – you are the essence of Love, made in the image of the Love that birthed you. You are pure conscious awareness. You are limitless and free. You do not need to become more than you are. You are already all that you are seeking.

This is the great dilemma in which you find yourself. You continue to believe that you can find what you are yearning for outside yourself, and all the while, the great peace and love you seek lies within you. We say to you 'Stop seeking!' and yet still you look for what you want where it is not. It is your belief in separation that is limiting you. You believe yourself to be a separate body, apart from all other bodies, essentially alone in this world. But there is only One – One God, One Life, One Consciousness. You yearn to

Chapter 12: The Flight of the Eagle

know Oneness even as you cling to your belief in separation. To know the Oneness of all life you must wake up to who you really are and know in each moment that you and your Father are One – created and Creator, inseparable.

You have forgotten who you are. You have believed yourself to be insignificant, small and obscure. Are there not billions of other souls on this planet now? Even as you experience yourself as the centre of your universe, do you not feel that you are as a tiny grain of sand unnoticed in a sea of sand? Each child of God is precious in the eyes of the Father. Each is known and loved. Each has a purpose to fulfil, a role to play in this great drama called life. Each is an essential thread in the great and beautiful tapestry being woven by the Creator.

You yearn to awaken, to be at one with all life, and yet this goal seems elusive. It is as though you reach out to grasp it, and all you find is empty air. In your disappointment, you try yet harder 'to get it'. As if there was something 'to get'. You are It now. You are all you can ever be. You are waiting for some great moment of transformation that will change your world. There is no switch that you can press 'on' that will suddenly initiate this change. All that is required is a realisation of the Truth.

Know that Love is your essence, but if fear arises, feel it. Do not disparage it. Welcome it and love it and embrace it as you would a lost child. It is in extending love that you will find the happiness and fulfilment for which you long. You will experience joy when you choose to be the Love which you are – when you choose to be your Self. The truth is so simple, but you pass it by, believing that awakening must be a complex process. You overlook the very thing that you are seeking and turn again to sources outside yourself for answers. Come home to your Self. Simply love. Be at peace with what is and look upon all that you see with soft eyes and an open heart.

THE ASCENDENCE OF LOVE

The eagle, as it ascends in the skies, does so effortlessly. It does not struggle. It does not fear. It allows itself to be uplifted by the movement of warm air as it floats high above the Earth. The body of the eagle is strong, but it exerts no effort. Its wings are wide open, and it is raised up joyously. Visualise the eagle above you now. Feel within you the grandeur and beauty of its form as you see it soar over the countryside. Feel the power and strength of its wings, which are open to the movement of air through its feathers. Be One with the eagle now. Sense the trust in which it abides. It does not fret over what is past. It does not worry about what is to come. It simply is. It is the expression of Love in form. Beautiful and powerful, its presence on the planet is a gift to be honoured.

There are many roads leading into the Light. Some roads are muddy and marred by potholes. Others are littered with obstacles, great boulders that must be surmounted. Some lead you through dark tunnels and carry you past scenes of devastation and suffering. But there is one road that is evenly paved and is illuminated by a gentle light. As you walk this road you feel the loving presence of those of us who walk with you, offering you our guidance and a steady hand when your footsteps waver. You choose which road you will follow, for you never cease to be responsible for what you experience. Will you choose to travel a hazardous road, or will you walk the road that is evenly paved and free of obstacles?

Love in Truth has always governed this world. The little bumps in the road, the periods of darkness, the illusion of suffering – can these not be a gift of Love? Do not go chasing after things that prove worthless when you grasp them. Stop. Stop and look at what you hold in your hands right now. Look at what is gifted to you. You need nothing more. You have everything. You are everything. No experience is worth the loss of the awareness of your Self. No experience need be sought to give the small self what it has hungered for.

Chapter 12: The Flight of the Eagle

You are waking up out of the dream. If you feel uncertain, know this is merely the ego's fear of dissolution. Realise that waking up to Reality is not difficult. And yet you have believed it to be so. It is only your resistance to *what is* that leads you down roads that present you with needless challenges. For have you not suffered enough? Have you not doubted, questioned, and struggled enough? Are you ready to stop all seeking and striving, and become as the eagle, and move through life freely and effortlessly? Your resistance is born of believing what is false. Your beliefs distort your perception, and you have failed to see the reality of the Heaven that is available to you in every moment.

Beloved friends, abandon all your old beliefs – *all* of them – and surrender into the loving arms of the Father who birthed you. These beliefs have not served you. They have not set you free from your self-created prison. Look honestly at all the beliefs you hold and question their reality. Indeed, you are not asked to *believe* anything. You are asked, simply, to be that which you are. You are asked to love, and in loving you will receive all that you could desire. Love is not a tangible object. It is not a thing to be sought. It is what you are always. It is only in loving that you will find freedom. It is only in loving that you will know the deep joy of fulfilment. The idle pleasures that you pursue in this world will never feed your soul as does the simple and precious joy of extending heartfelt love to the world. And in extending your love, you will find the connectedness you have sought with all of Creation. And you know it is not apart from you, because it *is* you. The lie of separation has been exposed, and you are set free.

The eagle is indeed a powerful creature, broad of wingspan and with talons strong and dexterous. In the wild the bird flies free at great heights. But there are eagles you have domesticated and taught to do your bidding. Eagles reared in captivity have become accustomed to being handled and have been trained to fly away and return to rest on an outstretched arm. They have come to accept the limitations of their restricted life. And this is what you have done to yourself.

You have lost sight of your true nature and have come to believe in the solidity of the walls you have constructed that limit you and restrict your view of the opportunities that lie beyond those walls. Your social conditioning has taught you that your limiting beliefs are true and your fear of stepping beyond those walls is justified. Consider which eagle lives the richer life: the wild eagle that flies free or the captive bird whose freedom is restricted? One is free and responsible for her own life, and the other is controlled and dependant. The soul of the wild bird soars to great heights as her wings carry her high into the skies. The captive bird knows her food source is secure, but she does not know the freedom of the unconfined and the unfettered. Which eagle would you rather be?

Are you willing to take responsibility for your experience? Will you commit to knocking down the walls of limitation you have built around you? Or will you be content to stay in the constricted arena of those walls? If you do not wish to step beyond these boundaries, ask yourself why. Are you using them to hide behind? Are you being governed by fear? Do you see yourself as unworthy or incapable? You look with awe upon the eagle in flight because you glory in its power and freedom. Will you not love yourself enough to claim your own freedom and power?

The days of limitation on this planet are numbered. The New Earth will blossom into a world where you can take flight and soar like the wild eagle to great heights, a planet free of constriction and control. Those who walk the New Earth will not know limitation or fear. The shackles of dependency on old beliefs will be unlocked, and the heart will know the joy and wonder of the innocent as each brother and sister steps out to explore the blessed sphere of the ascended planet. The thought of limitation will no longer be in

Chapter 12: The Flight of the Eagle

their memory banks. The concept of lack will not be present in their consciousness. They will not know fear because they will know the reality of Love.

Such is the promise offered those of you who are ready to step free from your prison cell and embrace your reality as Christ. If you choose to remain in the constricting cell you created, your choice will be honoured. You have been granted free will to do just whatsoever you desire to do. But contemplate the life of an eagle in the wild. Visualise the great bird in flight. Feel the majesty of its bearing as it lands on a high rocky shelf where its nest is built. Sense the intensity of its gaze and the clarity of its vision as it watches the world in silence. Feel the quietness within its being as it looks out upon the world below.

Consider this choice wisely. It is not a decision to be made idly, because the ramifications of this decision are great. Do you wish to walk in freedom, living as the Christ that you are? Or do you wish to stay wandering in a dream of dramas and discord? What you see within you will be projected outwards. Only as you discover the truth of your being and come to know the Love that is your essence, will you be able to walk the planet as Christ Incarnate.

The Earth is ascending and will no longer tolerate the disharmony and dissension that have troubled her lands. Now powerful geographical movements and changes in weather patterns are being enacted on the planet. This is simply change occurring, and this change is cause for celebration. You are called on to ascend with your Earth Mother. You can decide now to awaken to your reality as Christ and step into a happy dream. Will you choose to soar like the eagle into the heights of freedom, and know the ecstatic joy of living as the Love that you are? My beloved friends, choose wisely.

God's Child is Sinless

Fear is the dark and desolate bastion you have created to house the ego, and the ego strengthens the walls of this fortress to maintain its control over the mind. Yet neither the ego nor the fear born out of the belief in separation are real. The concept of separation has led you on many false trails and given you glimpses of hell. Fear has gripped you in a vice of confusion and blinds you to what is real and right before you now.

When fear dominates your thinking, how can you free yourself from its grasp? You must want to be free and intend it. Breathe deeply and begin to sense the peace that lies within. Commit to choosing a different path and be willing to make the choice for Love. You have only to make the decision to trust what unfolds in your life and allow all things to be as they are. If you seem to be faced with insurmountable problems, offer them up to the Holy Spirit, and let them go completely. Each time a dark thought would reappear in the mind, give it up to the Comforter, and trust in His guidance. Remember that you are not the director of your life and have no need to control anything. You are never alone and always is help available to you.

You call all things to you, and you are never a victim, even when fear engulfs you. While you may not consciously believe you have a choice as to what you experience, you know you can always choose *how* you will experience the events of your life. You have come to dread fear itself, but do not make yourself a victim of your own fear. It remains an illusion. Though the ego would strive to convince you of its reality, at all times you have the power to rise above it and rest in the Peace of God.

You are as God created you to be. You are Perfect Love, always. Never are you apart from the Father. Though you have come to believe in a separate self, there is no individualised ego. There is only the choice for Heaven or hell, Reality or illusion, sanity or insanity. When you awaken from the dream of an individualised ego, you will see that there is only One: One God and One Creation. You will recognise your Self in all you look upon, and you will realise that there is nothing outside of you or apart from you. You will know that there is only God.

What is it then, that disguises the Truth as images of separate bodies and objects? Why did the Son of God come to believe in the concept of separation, and become spellbound by the world constructed upon that belief? When the dark thought of separation arose in the mind of the Son, he looked upon it and became lost within it. He came to believe that it was real. And that thought – and it was but a thought – gave rise to guilt. The pain of that guilt was such that it was denied and projected outwards. But because there is only One Mind and there is nothing outside of you, the guilt that you appear to have pushed away from you simply became unconscious. This unconscious guilt has weighed heavily upon you and led you into a hell of your own making. All the worlds you have created have been built upon your belief in separation and the unconscious guilt you hold within you.

It is time now to rid yourself of these ancient demons and let Love heal the wounds of self-punishment which you have continually recreated because you have believed that you are capable of sin. Sin is not possible. How could the Holy Son of God commit a sin when

Chapter 13: God's Child is Sinless

he is created by the Father in the image of Himself? Because the Father creates only that which is like unto Himself, you are perfect and whole, and incapable of sin. Abandon the great seriousness you have abided in for aeons. Own your innocence and your power to live as the Christ that you are.

I love you, and I see only the Light that you are. I see your beauty and your innocence, and I know the power and the wisdom that resides within you. This you will see too, when you embrace your reality as Christ. I remind you again that this is not hard to do. It is but a choice away. Forgive yourself for all that you have judged within yourself. Forgive your projections upon your brothers and sisters. Forgive the world for out picturing the events you have judged to be distressful. Forgive your God for that which you have judged Him to be responsible. But above all, forgive yourself. For though it seems necessary to forgive all that appears to be outside of you, this is but an act of self-forgiveness. Because there is nothing outside of you, you have only, ultimately, to forgive your Self.

Precious children of God, forgive yourself wholly, and embrace your innocence. Abandon your guilt. Let it no longer cloud your perception and rob you of the peace for which you crave. Give up the need to punish yourself in all the many ways you have devised to torment and torture yourself because you believe you are capable of sin. You punish yourself mentally, by confusing the mind with fractious and conflicting thoughts. You punish yourself emotionally by wallowing in anxiety and grief and despair. And at times you punish yourself physically by creating pain and illness. Give up wanting to punish yourself any longer.

See the futility and insanity of nursing old guilts and self-blame. This is hell itself. Will you not now walk free of your hell and enter the portals of Heaven? We who watch over you will celebrate your arrival and welcome you into the realm of Peace with glad and grateful hearts. Sin is an egoic delusion. I did not preach of sin because sin is impossible to conceive in the children of God. A God of Love does not see error. He does not create in error. He looks upon you and sees only the glorious Light that you are.

I too walked this planet and came to know the pain and pleasures that are experienced during the life of a physical body. I am no different from you, for I too knew the conflicts and uncertainties you know. I am your brother and your friend, and I am not special. What I have accomplished, you too can accomplish. I committed to following the guidance of the Holy Spirit, just as you can. I chose to love and to forgive. I saw the pain and insanity of projection and blame and gave up the desire to judge my brothers and sisters. Though it seems that I have gone before you, yet we remain as One, and my journey has thus become your journey. It is done. You have reached the end of the road. You have no further distance to travel. You have only to realise this.

You are, in Truth, recreating in your mind what is already past. It is as though you were watching a movie filmed long ago and have become so immersed in it that you have forgotten who you are or where you are. The movie is not real. It is just images appearing on the screen of your mind. Wake up to what is Real. Stand up, step out of the movie theatre and walk free. You have sat in many movie theatres, watched many movies, but none of them were real. Nothing can keep you captivated by a movie but your own choice. So, will you not choose peace and freedom over drama and limitation? Will you not let Love be your guide and abandon all illusions of weakness and suffering? Heaven will come to Earth, and the Son of God will awaken to the reality of Love. Will you not choose this now?

When we speak of Heaven coming to Earth, what do we mean? The nightmare through which you have been wandering will be transmuted into the happy dream. Peace and Love will bloom upon the Earth. The Earth will reflect Reality. Is this not a joyous picture to contemplate? The dream of time and space as you now experience it will be transformed into a dream that reveals the Truth of the Kingdom. Delusions of drama and discord, pain and suffering, will be no more. Be willing now to let go of all the grave seriousness that has weighed upon you, and step lightly and joyously through the gateway into the peace of the New Earth.

Love is not a thought. It is the essence of who you are. It can be felt but is not something you can accurately describe. It is not something you can analyse and interpret. It is above and beyond the mind. You cannot think it, but you can be it. The heartfelt love that uplifts you into the quietness of deep joy is a feeling that you will come to value above all the emotions of pleasure brought forth by the ego. Love appears like a powerful energy that washes over you and through you, gently caressing you with the precious Peace of God. When the awareness of this Love fills your consciousness, it requires no effort to extend it to your brothers and sisters. And when you abide in this place of Love, your brothers and sisters will sense it in you and find rest and quiet joy in your presence.

Guilt is a useless emotion, because it will not lead you into the place of stillness where Love abides. Guilt will lead you away from Love, along false trails. Because it carries you into the darkness of false perceptions of unworthiness and wrongdoing, it ushers you away from the peace that will bring you clarity and comfort, the precious peace that lies ever within you. When the mind is no longer chattering frantically, when it is not striving desperately to find answers, you can let your awareness sink beneath the noise of the thinking mind and enter the silence within. For silence is the gateway into the deep peace of God that you crave, the peace that is beyond all comprehension.

Look upon the events of your life and observe where you are still holding on to old guilt that continues to weigh upon your spirit. Bring into your mind the awareness of each member of your earthly family, each friend, old and new, that you have encountered during your life, and each soul you have judged to be an enemy. Address each child of God, one by one, with heartfelt honesty and sincerity, and ask for their forgiveness. When emotions arise, as they will, feel them fully. You ask for their forgiveness, not because you have sinned, for that is not possible. You ask for their forgiveness because you are still nursing guilt within you and wish to forgive yourself.

Recognise that the one you are visualising is but an aspect of your Self, who has come into your life to offer to you the gift of Love's Presence to reveal you to yourself. As you address each brother and sister personally, express your sorrow for any pain you appear to have caused them, any judgement you have projected upon them, and any way you feel you have failed them. Then feel gratitude for their presence in your life. Give thanks for the opportunities of self-awareness they have presented to you. Remember that the essence of who you both are is Love, and feel your love flow outwards to them, embracing them gently. Whisper the words 'I love you' and set yourself free.

If you feel resistance to extending love to a brother, observe yourself honestly. Is there some latent anger yet lingering within? Have you failed to recognise that he stands before you as your Self? If you would heal this resistance, what can you do? You need to forgive, and forgive again, and forgive yet again. You do not realise how much tension you create in the body, and how much guilt is induced in the mind when you judge another. For how can you judge a brother without judging yourself for your condemnation of him? He is a holy and innocent child of God, come to the planet to reveal to you areas within your consciousness that are in need of healing. He is not apart from you. He is your Self reflected back to you. As you choose to see him, you will see yourself. Forgive him wholly and abandon the old habit of projection and blame. Choose to love him, if you would know self-love. Choose to see the Light of Christ

Chapter 13: God's Child is Sinless

that is in him, if you would see this in yourself.

Your self-judgement of your own actions has given rise to guilt. So too do you judge the physical appearance of the body. When it displeases you, you fear losing the approval of others. When you look into a mirror and condemn what you observe, you are seeing yourself as a body. You allow your perception of the body to rob you of peace. This is insanity. When you look at the reflection, you are observing an image that appears in the mind as shape and colour. This is not who you are. Remember that you are Consciousness Itself. You are pure Spirit. The body you dreamed up can be used as an instrument to extend Love, but you have used it in ways that deny you peace.

You look upon the body and you judge it as inadequate. It is an indication of the old falsehood you have clung to – 'I am not good enough, not attractive enough, not pleasing enough.' It is a lie! Do not believe it. You are divine. You have been created as the Father created you to be: good, perfect, whole, lovable, beautiful, and cherished. You are Christ Incarnate. What can be grander than this? You are made in the image of the Father, and you are infinitely precious. Abandon all notion that you are anything less than you were created to be. When you look into a mirror, trust what you see. Let no thought of limitation, of not being good enough, restrict your joy and fulfilment. Love what you see. Be the Love that you are and let love shine away the darkness of all guilty and self-disparaging thoughts.

The bells have rung out. The Father is calling His children home. It is time to step out of the darkness of your fear and unconscious guilt and into the Light of Truth. Give up your belief in separation. Know, with your whole being, that you are One with all of Creation. There is only God. All that is, is God, and God is all that is. You live God. You breathe God. And because this is so, Love is your essence. Love is the only thing that is real, and it can never be imperilled. Love then, your Self, and all that you look upon. Love the morning sun as it rises in the sky over Mother Earth and love the birds that sing in celebration of the dawning of a new world. Love your brothers and sisters and see the Light of Christ shining forth from them. Above all, love your God, the Father who created you in the image of Himself. And joyously celebrate the awakening of the Son of God from the dream of separation that has kept him in bondage for too long.

Awakening

The time of awakening is upon you. This is not because it is being forced upon you, but because you have called it to you. *You have chosen to come into incarnation at this time of great change*, when Mother Earth herself is rising into a new vibration. The New Earth is being born, and this is cause for celebration. The planet itself will no longer tolerate the energies of chaos and suffering. As she rises out of the shadows of the old world, scenes of disorder are manifesting on the planet. Old discordant social structures created out of fear are giving way to the new that are shaped by the hands of Love. Now Love is on the ascendence.

You are not separate from your Father: you are Love Itself. And you are One with all life. You are the one who has cried out to the Father that you are ready to put aside the playthings of childhood and step into your adult role as the Awakened Christ. You are the one who is even now reaching your hand out to your Maker, asking to be drawn up out of the illusion into the Light. Your plea has been heard. The Father sees only that which you are, and He knows that you are in Truth already awake. And yet in response to your call, He has sent out His runners, aspects of your Self, to lead you back home to Him.

When you read a holy manuscript that speaks of God's Truth, know not that this is outside of you. It is your Self speaking to you. It is your Self that is dragging the veils of illusion from your eyes. All the ancient wisdom that tells of the reality of Love is your wisdom, ever-present within you. Think not that awakening is a difficult task. It calls only for a change of perception. It only requires you to make the choice for Love, the choice for Peace, in every moment. Have I not told you that the way is easy and the burden light? Your perceptions of difficulties and burdens are illusory. Put aside now all the fairy tales you have believed to be real. No longer believe the stories you have told yourself about your problems and your weakness and your helplessness. Leave them in the past where they belong. They are but the delusions of an ego that thrived on fear.

It is time to recognise your power - it comes to you from the Father, not from somewhere outside of you. It is ever-present within you. It is the energy that resides in the depths of your being. You are the manifestation of Love Itself, and Love is the power of God that moves within you and through you. Beloved friends, own your power now. Place it in the forefront of your awareness. You are not limited by time and space, and nor are you small, weak and helpless. You are the greatness of God made manifest upon the Earth. All power under Heaven and Earth is yours because it comes to you of the Father.

Dwell no longer upon illusions. Come home to the Truth of your being. Come home to God. You did not come to this planet to play at being imprisoned by fear. You did not come to act as a blind, weak, constricted being, bound by the form of a body. You came to shine, to extend the love that you are out into the world created in error. You came to enact the Will of God.

In this moment you can put the past behind you and break free from the illusion of hell. Do not linger in the past. Do not continue to recreate it in your mind. Let it go. Come to me now and walk with me into the Light. And as we walk together, we will shine the Light that we are out into the world. Thus, will we bring healing to the

Chapter 14: Awakening

world, and beckon our brothers and sisters back into the fold of our Father's Presence.

Every act of love performed radiates its beauty out into the whole of Creation. Not one precious act of love goes unseen or unfelt. When love is extended, it blesses the whole of the Creation. And when you extend love to your brothers and sisters, you are offering love to yourself. All that you give do you receive. As Love radiates out from you, it will heal the wounds that have festered in the darkness of fear. It will caress the brow of the one weary of struggle and longing for home. And it will remind the souls that yet sleep in the realm of dreams, that Love is the only reality, and Truth is ever-present within them.

Beloved friends, trust not the dictates of fear. Trust only in Love and recognise the power that comes to you from the Father. Only as you trust in the Father's Will can you come to know the freedom and joy for which you long. It is only to be found when you realise that you have no life outside the Father. There can be no greater happiness than this: to love your Father with all your heart, and all your mind and all your soul, and to feel His Love radiating back to you in every moment, through every experience, from every brother and sister you encounter. For this is the only Reality. This is the only Truth that can be known. And thus, are you blessed, and bring this blessing to the whole of Creation.

Let go and give up the control of your life to the One who birthed you. For you, who have believed yourself to be separate from your Maker, know not what this moment is for. You would use it for your own purposes, to gain what you believe you need. When you come to see that in fulfilling the Father's Will, you will know all that you need will be given unto you. You can thus relinquish the desire to control your world, and trust in the Father's Love to guide you in all that you do.

Nothing of value is to be gained by 'efforting', by desperately searching and struggling for what you thought you needed. The Father knows what will be required by you to fulfil His Plan, and He will freely give unto you all that you ask for when you commit your life to Him. There is nothing you will lack, and nothing you need fear. You have but to give up all efforts to control or plan your life. And in thus giving up control and surrendering to the Father's Will, you are set free.

I say unto you, the way *is* easy. Give all your burdens unto me, and if you feel your footsteps falter, reach out for my hand and I will steady you. I am never apart from you, so do not think that I am far from you. If you believe yourself to be alone, realise that this is a deceptive ploy of the ego that would strive to convince you that this is possible. You are never alone. Always do I walk with you. How could it be otherwise when there is only One? There is but One Life, One God, One Creation.

Because I am never apart from you, I am always available to join with you as you travel on your journey into the Light. I love you, and I willingly walk at your side to share your journey because I love you. See me not as apart from you, for I am indeed that aspect of your Self that you have called into your consciousness now to remind you of what is always true. Do you not recognise me as your Self? Do you not realise that I am present on your Heart always? Do not deny my presence within you. Know that I am you, and because I have awakened into the Kingdom of Heaven, so too have you. Abandon all thought of separation now and walk with me along the road that holds no obstacles, where walking is effortless.

When you feel the Reality of Love in your Heart, it will shine from your eyes and speak through your words and bless with the touch of your hand. You will become a Light unto the world, and your light will bring healing to those longing for peace. Because Love is the only reality, it is only Love that can heal. If you would heal the world, you have but to bring Love to it. Love cannot be

Chapter 14: Awakening

forced upon a world that does not welcome it. Thus, do I say: Love waits upon your welcome. It comes quietly, with gentleness and compassion. It comes bearing gifts of wisdom and understanding. For Love allows all things and trusts all things. It knows that you cannot walk the pathway to the Kingdom bearing the instruments of coercion. Love works freely and effortlessly, knowing nothing of force or compulsion. Only the fearful use devices that would control and compel.

Awakening then is but Self-realisation. There is nothing you need do, nothing you need strive for, nothing you need learn. All that is required is that you take the blinkers from your eyes and recognise what has been within you all along. Love is ever-present. It is not something you must reach out for or grasp possessively to you. Love is who you are. You cannot find it outside of yourself, because it is not to be found. There is nothing outside of you. Realise the power of Love that is within you now. When you extend this love to your brothers and sisters, you discover that it was within you all along.

Whenever you look for love where it is not, you will feel frustrated by your failure to find it. What then? Will you search for it even more desperately? Or will you come to accept that your reality is Love, and realise the insanity of searching outside yourself for what was always within you as your Self? Beloved friends, *look not outside yourself*. Be at peace with who you are now, however you picture yourself. You are Love, and because Love is in your mind, the One Mind, all that you look upon is Love. All Creation emanates the Love of the Father, and mirrors back to you the Love that you are.

When you judge yourself, and guilt confuses the mind, you know not what you do. For how can you condemn the perfect creation of the Father? For surely, if you judge yourself, do you not cast doubt upon the wisdom of the Creator? Judge not yourself but come to see the Light of Christ that you are. Honour the Truth of who you are. Let not the delusions of a fearful mind lead you into the darkness of guilt and self-blame. Love yourself wholly, for until you do, you will not know the Kingdom of Heaven.

Know there is nothing that you can be but that which you are, and you are the presence of Love. Your essence is Love always. You do not have to prove your worth or your innocence. Love radiates from you as light streams forth from a radiant star. You have known guilt because you have judged past behaviours as 'wrong' or 'bad'. Love does not condemn. Only the ego would strive to persuade you that you are something other than that which you are in Truth.

Because you are the offspring of the Father, you express Love in all that you do and all that you say. You do not need to validate that which you are. Does a bird need to convince the world that it is a bird? It simply is. No matter what events take place within the dream, the Truth of you always loves. The dream is but a dream and has no reality. When you can move through the dream, knowing in every moment that Love is your essence, you will know that it is not possible for you to sin or hurt another. You will be in the world, but not of the world. Allow the dramas of the dream world to unfold before you without judgement. They are merely an illusion, a false image appearing on the screen of the mind. Never can they take from you what has been given to you by your Creator. Remember always that you are the Love of God made manifest.

Precious children of God, the time of awakening is here. Will you not now take up your cross and follow me into the Light? Will you not relinquish the dream and recognise the futility of judgement and condemnation? Will you not embrace your Reality as Christ? Because you remain as your Father created you to be, this is not an arduous task. It requires only that you choose to be the Love which you have always been.

When I ask that you take up your cross and follow me, I do so

Chapter 14: Awakening

knowing full well where I am leading you. And what is the cross that I bid you carry? It is the essence of Christ Mind, the symbol of the resurrection. Your churches have equated the cross with the Crucifixion, but though I was nailed to a cross, my purpose was to illustrate the power of the Son of God to overcome death and resurrect into the Kingdom of Heaven. Claim back the cross as the symbol of your power to overcome adversity and enter into the realm of peace and sanity. Cling no longer to any sense of victimhood. I was never a victim. All the images of me suffering on the cross are deceptive. I freely chose the path that I walked so that you might bear witness to the power of Love to overcome the pangs of the body and to triumph over death.

Just as I was never a victim, neither are you. Every step you take is chosen by you because this is what you have wanted to do. Will you not now choose to take each step in Love? Will you not cast from you all concept of crucifixion, and resurrect into the Kingdom of Heaven? I love you, and I know the longing in your heart for peace. I know that you are weary of walking the long dusty road that has been marred by discord and disharmony. So, take my hand now, grasp it firmly, and let me lead you out of the darkness into the Light. Your Father waits with open arms to welcome His Child unto Himself.

The End of Suffering

Your one responsibility is to accept the Atonement for yourself. Why is this so? Because when you accept that you are innocent and free, and One with all of creation, you will cease to project Christ outwards onto some being beyond yourself. You will embrace Christ as yourself. You are indeed Christ, One with the Father who birthed you. In Reality, you are not separate from anyone or anything. When I say to you that your brother is yourself, I speak only of what is true. You never look upon another but see only your Self. Therefore, do not linger in the illusory world of false perceptions. Embrace the truth of who you are, now and always. Take up your cross, the essence of your Christhood, and walk at my side, as my equal, into the Light of Truth.

You who appear to journey upon this planet in a body have never been limited by time and space. You are infinite and eternal. In any moment, you are not restricted to one dimension but span multiple dimensions. You experience time sequentially, but all is happening now, in the present moment. There is only now. There are multiple movies playing all at once. You have chosen to watch this particular movie, a movie playing out on planet Earth where you are the one born from the womb of an earthly mother and living out the span of a life until death greets the physical structure you call the body. You are watching it all replay in your mind.

THE ASCENDENCE OF LOVE

We have spoken of disorder and disharmony, of dramatic changes in weather patterns, and of the downfall of the old institutions built on a foundation of fear. This is but one of the movies being screened, a movie constructed by collective thoughts. If the collective mind would change, you would find yourself watching a different movie. The script is written, but there are multiple scripts for multiple movies. Therefore, never is suffering compulsory. You can rise up to a different dimension, and choose to watch a different movie, one based on unity and love and harmony.

It is important that you recognise that all suffering is wrought out of fear, and that you need not suffer. When I was nailed to the cross on Golgotha, I did not suffer. My awareness of my Father's Love was so all encompassing that I was not aware of suffering. Even as I was experiencing physical pain, I did not suffer. Do not equate physical pain with suffering. Pain is of the body; suffering is of the mind. All the images that decorate your churches that depict me suffering in anguish upon the cross are false. Does this in any way negate my message? Indeed not. I came to demonstrate the unreality of death, and the power of Love to overcome suffering. It is time for the world to embrace the Truth that I was not a victim at any time. I willingly fulfilled my role. I overcame suffering, just as I overcame death.

It is time that you recognised the power of Love to heal this world and committed to living Love in every moment. It is time to give up all desire to suffer. Recognise how you have clung to suffering because you have valued it. See how you have used suffering as a means to bring you what you thought you wanted. Because there are no accidents, and you are never a victim of the world you see, you are responsible for all you experience, including your suffering.

All the pain you have encountered, all the discord and disharmony you have witnessed, and all the agony of deep depression

Chapter 15: The End of Suffering

into which you have fallen – you are responsible for it all. When you suffer, accept that this is by your own choice. Do not project blame for this outside of you onto someone or something you have judged to be the cause. *You* are the cause of it all. Are you willing to take responsibility for this? Are you willing to see how much you have valued suffering? Can you accept that you have wanted and freely chosen all the despair and anguish you have experienced?

If tension and resistance are arising within you as you read these words, own them too as your creation. Embrace them innocently and observe honestly what they are revealing to you about yourself. Never deny or resist your resistance to hearing the truth expressed. Allow it to be, and look upon it with honesty, and see it for what it is. Do not allow great seriousness to weigh upon you. Look upon your reactions without judgement, with childlike wonder and acceptance.

Suffering is the illusion to which you have clung because you believed it to be real. You thought that suffering was necessary to assuage your guilt. All your guilt was born when the mad idea of separation arose in the mind of the Son. An idea is but a thought and has no reality. And yet you have come to believe so deeply in your guilt that you manifest suffering in an unconscious attempt to punish yourself for what you believed to be the sin of separating from your Father.

Your Father knows nothing of sin and has never judged His children. Cast from you any ancient beliefs that your God has punished you for your sins. How could it be possible for your Holy Father, who is but Love, to do anything other than create in Love? He created you in the image of Himself and sees only that which you are in Truth. The belief in sin is an insane belief. Only the insane could conceive of a loving God judging them and inflicting punishment upon them. It is not God who is punishing you. It is *you* punishing *yourself*. It is you who have believed that you have something to gain by suffering. But what can suffering bring you other than torment and confusion?

Look upon the suffering you have experienced during this lifetime and see it for what it is. You have believed suffering was real because you have believed you are a body. You may have believed it was necessary to suffer because you are convinced it has taught you compassion and understanding. Or perhaps you have believed you needed to suffer as karmic retribution for the suffering you caused others in the past. These are all just beliefs and are all illusory. Recognise how the power of your beliefs has structured your life and brought to you all the experiences you have encountered.

Realise that no suffering is necessary or even possible. You have just been lost in an insane dream. You are not a body and are in Truth incapable of suffering. When you realise that your reality is wholly Love, you will know that there is nothing you need learn or seek to become. When you accept that there is no past and no future, you will know that you need feel no guilt over what has been, nor need you worry about what is to come. When you abide wholly in the perfection of this present moment and embrace the Truth of who you are in Reality, you will perceive that there is nothing for which you need to suffer. You do not need to pay retribution for past errors. The past is gone. It is no more. This moment is ever birthed anew, and the past has no relevance to what is occurring now. It need not impinge upon you unless you bring it with you into the present moment. Therefore, abandon your belief in karmic debts, and all perception that you need to suffer in any way for what has occurred in the past.

While you fail to accept your Reality as Love and continue to believe that there is something you need to learn, you will be convinced that you yet need to become more than you are: kinder or wiser, more loving or more caring. Please come to realise that you are all you can be – right now. There is nothing – *nothing* – that you need to learn. It is this fallacy that keeps you locked in the cycle of

Chapter 15: The End of Suffering

seeking and striving. Hear me again – *there is nothing you need to learn or to become.* You are everything you want to be – right now.

You do not need to be more loving. You do not need to be more compassionate and understanding. You do not need to wake up because you are already awake. When you justify your suffering by professing that it has taught you to be kinder and have more empathy and understanding for others, I will say to you that you could only be convinced of this if you believed that you were a separate body, alone and apart from other bodies. When you accept the Atonement for yourself, you will know yourself as Christ, perfect and whole, birthed by a loving God, created in His own image.

My precious brothers and sisters, do you not see the Truth that I am expressing to you? You do not need to suffer any longer. You do not need to experience guilt any longer. The separation never occurred. You are eternally One with your God. You need no longer wander aimlessly through the dream, believing it to be real. You are free now. You have always been free. Are you willing to accept this, and abandon all your false perceptions of need and lack and limitation? Beloved children of God, it is time. Wash from your eyes the last remnants of sleep and look upon the world anew. Look upon it with great love and acceptance of what is. And as you offer this to the world, so it will be returned to you abundantly.

If you find that suffering still holds some attraction for you, ask yourself why this is so. Are you yet feeling guilty and need to punish yourself? Why would you wish to punish yourself if you knew that sin was impossible? You could only believe this of yourself if you failed to recognise who you are in Reality. Do you still believe that you need to suffer to learn and grow? This belief is deceptive. Suffering is an old habit, but it has brought you no joy. For joy is born of Love, not fear. If you would know the sweetness of joy, be willing to give up your attachment to suffering. Be willing to see how it has led you down alleyways which lead nowhere, into dark corners that have constricted you. You may think you can hide from the Truth by escaping into suffering, but the Truth remains as a brilliant star that will shed Light into all those dark corners and guide you back out of blind alleys.

Do you see pain as a familiar companion that permits you to avoid what you do not want to see? Do you use suffering as an escape into an illusory world? Does suffering give you justification to remain small, weak, and helpless, a victim of something you perceive to be outside of you? Look upon your reactions honestly, and do not deceive yourself when you make the decision to suffer. For it is always a decision, and at no time do you need ever suffer as a helpless victim of the world.

Because there is only One – One Life, One God, One Creation – and you are that One, you are responsible for it all: all the pain you create for yourself, the discord and disharmony that manifests among family and friends, the dramas you see enacted on your television screens. Do not separate yourself from any of it, because it is not separate from you. It is all you, because there is only One. We do not express this truth idly, because we would have you come to live as that One. Be therefore that which you are. Recognise the Oneness of all creation and know that you are that One. Know that you are the Light of the world.

You can look upon the dream you created in error and see that it is but a dream and has no power over you. You can bring all your suffering to an end: bury it deeply, and let it dissolve away in the soil of the past. I would not have you suffer any longer. I would not have you deceive yourself by believing you are guilty of sin and need to punish yourself for your errors of perception. I would have you know that you are infinitely precious and are dearly loved. You are born of Love, and Love is all that you are.

If suffering in any form manifests in your life, accept that you are holding onto false concepts and be willing to give up this ancient belief in anguish and affliction, torment and torture. Offer up your suffering unto me and call upon the Comforter to guide you out of the darkness of illusory thoughts. For it is your thoughts and beliefs that cause you to suffer. It is your interpretation of events that leads you to judge your experience and find fault with the world you see. Only if you believe you are worthy of suffering, can you experience suffering. Only if you believe that it is possible for you to be hurt, can you be hurt. Only if you believe another can cause you pain, can you experience another causing you pain.

When it appears that you are suffering, when you seem to be distressed or entrapped in a painful ordeal, recognise that this is an opportunity – an opportunity to elect to suffer no more, to see that you have believed the thoughts that have been dominant in your mind, and you need simply choose again. Thoughts are but thoughts, opinions you have come to believe express the Truth. They are not real. Realise the insanity of any thoughts that would convince you of the reality of suffering. Can you now see that suffering is neither necessary nor possible? Are you willing to acknowledge that suffering is an illusion? When you finally come to accept this truth, you will be free to live as the Christ that you are.

All-that-Is is created by the Hands of Love and remains an expression of Love. Look upon your world with the eyes of Christ and see the great light shining from within all things. God's Creation is One, not many. God's Creation is whole, not fragmented. God's Creation is joyous, not grim and despairing. Remember this truth, and you will be set free from all suffering.

The Pathway of Remembrance

Beloved children of God, now is the time of remembrance. It is time to put aside all the things of the past that have troubled you and led you down false pathways into darkness. Now is the time to acknowledge who you are in Truth. And are you not of the Light? Are you not the Holy Child of God, come forth to heal the wounds of disillusionment and discord that have been rife upon this planet? My beloved brothers and sisters, put aside all your grievances and remember what alone is true. You are Light, you are Love, and you are ever One with the Father.

It matters not what language you speak, what colour the skin of the body, nor even what you believe. It matters not if you have abandoned all hope of a loving God that will support you and protect you. It matters not if you feel alienated from all thought of a life beyond this world. It matters not if you believe you are merely this body you seem to inhabit and that you will cease to be when the body dies. These are simply beliefs, thoughts that parade through the mind. They do not determine who you are in Truth. What is real cannot be threatened. Light will always shine away the darkness and Truth will overcome illusion.

You have believed in suffering, and because you have done so, you have suffered. But suffering is not obligatory. It is not necessary, nor is it helpful. For while you believe in suffering, you create reasons to suffer and justify your beliefs by convincing yourself that you gain thereby. You think that suffering teaches you compassion. You think it makes you worthy of growth and understanding. In Reality there is nothing you need to understand. When you realise who you are in Truth, you will realise that you do not need to 'grow'. You have but to *be* – to be the Love that you are, to extend the Love that you are, to shine the Light that you are out upon this world.

This will seem like blasphemy to some. What – not grow? Not learn to be better that I am? Not rise to higher levels of consciousness? Do you not see that the whole idea of a hierarchy of consciousness is a denial of your Oneness with God, your equality with all of God's creations? Many are confused about this concept of growth. Do you not see that it is only a concept, an idea to describe a process. In Reality there is no process. There is only God expressing the Love that God is. It is all in the realm of mind that the worlds you experience are constructed, world upon world, dreamt up to experience and savour. Does that mean that they are real and that you are trapped within them? No, indeed not. They are simply an aspect of the dream. That does not make them real. A dream remains a dream.

Does this mean that the concept of growth is not useful? Indeed, it is useful, because you are waking up by degrees. You are learning to remember who you are in Reality. It is a learning process, a gradual re-awakening to the Truth. This occurs because fear still has a stranglehold upon your mind and it is necessary to rouse you from your stupor slowly and steadily, to avoid retraction into the darker spheres of egoic thinking. Do not struggle to understand this but let these thoughts filter into the mind to avoid creating resistance to them.

Embrace the Truth that you and the Father are One. Recognise how your beliefs are limiting you and keeping you wandering along false pathways through a maze of continual learning and striving.

Chapter 16: The Pathway of Remembrance

Give up the struggle. Let go of the perceived need to improve yourself, to be something better than you are now. You do not need to keep striving towards that elusive goal of enlightenment. It has already been attained. You are enlightened now. It is the ego – and you are not the ego – that continually strives for what always seems out of reach. It is the ego that uses the whole drama of striving and struggle to maintain its stranglehold on your mind.

Beloved friends, stop right now and look about you. It matters not where you appear to be. Simply look upon what you see and recognise the choices that you have made to bring you to this place. Never are you a victim of what you see and experience. Ever are you the master of your experience. You decide how you will respond to all that occurs. If you are happy or unhappy, it is because you have made a decision to feel this way. If you suffer or do not suffer it is by your choice.

Even though we have spoken of this often, are there not times when you fall into the old habit of believing that what is outside of you is the cause of what you feel? This tendency to slip into illusion calls for greater commitment to remembering what is true. Be diligent and let no thought of victimhood cloud your mind. When you are not at peace, know that some thought of discord, of judgement, of mistrust, has entered your awareness. When this has occurred you have the opportunity to choose again, to choose Love, to choose peace, to choose to trust in who you are in Truth.

The way of the Teacher of Righteousness is the way I ask you to travel. It is that way walked by others before you, those that found peace in the presence of the divine wisdom that Love represents. It is the way of the great masters who have gone before you and prepared the path to make easy your way. Will you not follow them? As you look about you and see the place from which you have come, can you not recognise the great potential of this moment to step out on this pathway, at peace, certain of the great joy to be found along this way. The great mystery that God is – it is calling to you now, beckoning you onwards into the heart of all that the Father is.

We do not ask great deeds of you. We do not ask you to struggle and suffer for some great cause. You are not asked to seek for anything. There is *nothing* to strive for. You do not have to create great waves upon the planet. You do not have to save the world. There is nothing you need to fix. You do not need to seek for some greater ambition, some magnificent task to accomplish to honour your God. Simply remember that *you* are the purpose, *you* are the meaning, *you* are the great Light illuminating the world with your light and your love.

The pathway of remembrance is a simple path, a gentle path, a path that lies open before you now. It calls to you to remember what alone is true. It calls to you to realise that only Love is real and that this Love is the essence of your being. It calls to you to recognise that separation is a lie, and you are never apart from the Source of your being.

Fear may still have a place in your mind, but fear is not your enemy. It represents a misappropriation of the power of thought, the power to create. When you abide in the truth that Love is the great power that lies at the heart of all you see, you will begin to trust that all is indeed well. Recognise that all that you fear that seems to be outside of you is merely a projection of your fear of yourself. When you stop feeding this fear and realise its unreality, you will be open to experience the great power of Love at work in your life. Choose then the path of remembrance. Choose to step out boldly onto this path that is blessed by Love and let it draw you onwards into the Light.

Look at the ways that fear has quietly, unknowingly, found expression in the things that you think and do... Denial... Avoidance... Projection of blame... Self-judgement... Disillusionment with what is... Loneliness... Struggling to achieve... Look about you and

Chapter 16: The Pathway of Remembrance

recognise that before you lies the opportunity to shine, to be the Truth of who you are. Whenever questions arise in your mind, know there is only one answer: respond with love. Love is the answer to every dilemma, every uncertainty. There are no set rules in the Book of Love. Here there are no rigid expectations. Love does not exert control and instil fear. It frees and unites. It uplifts. It rejoices. Yes, it may call on you to climb to great heights, and sometimes to wield a hammer to smash through old conventional structures, but do not fear to act as your heart dictates. Let all the 'shoulds' and 'musts' fall by the wayside. Simply listen to your heart for it will guide you faithfully. Do not judge yourself or others for the choices made. Let be what is, and let Love be your way-shower.

The time of awakening *is* at hand. So close now. And if at times you despair and feel yourself far from us and the Truth, know that this is merely the ego's ploy to distract you because it fears its own demise. As you claim your divinity you are set free. Only your own mind can enslave and imprison you, and you are always the master of your mind. Always do you have the power to choose but you have become bewitched by your own creations, believing the illusions you created to be real and denying your great power and strength to overcome adversity.

You have painted the scenes on the canvas of your life, and if you will, *you* can change them by recognising your capability to seize the paintbrush and paint the scenes anew. You have never been helpless. You are not a victim of anyone or anything. Yes, you live in a society that has taught you to abide by its rules and to conform to its expectations of behaviour. But you can rise above this. You can realise that you are free – ever free – and can make choices that are based on the Truth and not on lies. This is your power. It is the power of the Love that abides within you. Claim it now. Acknowledge the God that lives within you, as you, and through you. When you do so, you will know no greater joy or fulfilment.

THE ASCENDENCE OF LOVE

The peace that emanates from those that walk this path of remembrance is a balm to those that enter their presence. Peace is the natural state of those who recognise their Oneness with their Holy Father. This peace can penetrate the walls of resistance of those who have clung to the false perception that judgement and victimhood are justified. Peace, then, is the only goal worth pursuing. This peace is not to be gained by giving up your sovereignty. The Peace of God is quiet and strong. It is not born out of false submission, nor is it a deceptive means to control the course of events. Peace is born when all forms of control are relinquished, and you can let go and surrender to all that you are experiencing. It is the natural outcome when one surrenders to the Will of the Father and allows all to be as it is, without resistance. It arises not from tension but relaxation.

So let go. Simply that. Let go. Let go the fear, the concerns for the body, the concerns for the state of the planet, the concerns for your future. Whatever the fear that limits you, relinquish it to us. Let us carry this burden of uncertainty for you. Let go and let be. Do not doubt that all is indeed well, and it is only fear that would declare otherwise. And what is this fear but a creation of a mind that has forgotten the truth. Do not worry about what is to come. Remember that this is the moment in which you live. The tomorrow that you envisage can only be a figment of your imagination. Come, as I have bid you, to the edge of the cliff. It is beckoning to you now, urging you to make the leap into the unknown. Leap into the nothingness and be set free. Leap and know that we are with you as you do, urging you on into the Light, urging you to remember.

Those that have walked the path of remembrance and awakened to their reality as Christ wear an aura of serenity. This serenity is the balm that puts fears to rest, that turns the tables on the old-world paradigms that disturbed and troubled. It is the essence of Love, the essence of lightness, the essence of emptiness. It does not question, and it does not analyse. It does not judge or bewilder. It allows the

Chapter 16: The Pathway of Remembrance

soul to relax and release, to let go, to relinquish the old patterns of behaviour that brought tension to the body and confusion to the mind. So, the pathway of remembrance is the pathway of peace. It is the gentle road leading to union, to the recognition of Oneness, to the knowledge that the God of Love is alive in everything, even the very air you breathe. It leads to the acknowledgement that there is no separation, that all are One in Christ.

The days can be wearisome for those who have forgotten what is true and real. Tranquillity comes to those who remember who they are and why they have come to the planet at this time. Your purpose is to shine your light upon the world, to remind all of the truth of who they are, to extend the Love that you are out upon a world crying out for love. This is no small thing. This is the great purpose of the atonement: the revelation of the truth, the awakening of mankind from the dream, the shining away of darkness. For this reason have you come, to be the instrument of the Divine, to enact the power of God to heal and soothe and set free. This is indeed no small task, but it is one that will bring you great fulfilment and joy.

Those that walk this pathway are blessed. They know who they are and what their purpose is. They are happy and content. They do not fear recrimination or rejection. They do not doubt, and they do not question. For who would question what is unquestionable? Who would doubt what is so certain? It is Love unhindered that blesses them and comforts them. It is Love that lights up their eyes and brings warmth to their smiles. It is Love that leads them onwards on this pathway and assures them of their strength and vitality. They are free.

Freedom from Illusion

Peace is your rightful heritage, but it is not to be gained by struggle. It will not be achieved by fighting against those who rebel. It will not be won by warring against other nations. It will not be attained by punishing those who have broken the rules of your society and filling your prisons with these 'offenders'. Peace on Earth will only be made manifest when you enter into the Peace that lies within you, and you become the living presence of this peace upon the planet.

Those of you who will yet judge your brothers and sisters for what you deem to be their sins, turnabout, look upon yourself and question your judgements. What is it that you judge in others that you are afraid to recognise in yourself? They are the mirror that will reveal to you that which you have denied and avoided perceiving in your own thoughts and behaviours.

You who have belittled your brothers and sisters of a different age or gender, question your motivations. You who have condemned those of other cultures and religions, become aware of your beliefs and examine your judgements. You who have vilified others as criminals or paedophiles or terrorists, stop and peruse your own thoughts and feelings, and remember that all that you see is your projection. You cannot recognise in another what you have not known within yourself. Judgement and condemnation are never justified. Because you project only what you do not wish to own within yourself, we call on you to forgive *all*.

Forgive all that you condemn in others and forgive yourself for your projections upon them. Forgive your brothers and sisters, forgive yourself, and forgive your God. How can you know deep peace if you have not fully forgiven? What discord within you is calling out to be healed? How can you discern this? Your memories are not hidden away in some secret inaccessible vault. You can access all that you have previously experienced and bring into your conscious mind the grievances that await your forgiveness.

Recall the souls with whom you have had significant encounters in this lifetime. Honestly and openly, examine how you feel when you envision them. Let no hesitant welcome escape your awareness. Let no resistance, no feelings of awkwardness, no sadness or minor irritations elude you. Acknowledge the residual emotions that linger within you. To what judgements are you clinging? What are they mirroring to you? Own your full responsibility for your emotions and all you have experienced. With the Holy Spirit's guidance, visualise each soul and sense the thoughts and emotions that were present within them during your encounter. Forgive them and sense the peace of acceptance and the gentleness of compassion enter your awareness.

Peace rests gently in the heart of the one who has forgiven the world, and a peaceful heart is as a panacea that supports the healing of others. Peace is like a gentle stream that flows through the mind, eroding away the sharp edges of judgement and blame. For why would a soul at peace want the disharmony and discord that arise from false perceptions? Peace is the great blessing that sees no separation between your brothers and sisters, and no separation between your Self and God.

While you remain in judgement and hesitate to forgive, your projections will appear justified and freedom from illusion will

Chapter 17: Freedom from Illusion

not appear desirable. For the ego loves its dramas and clings to its sense of victimisation. You need to shift your awareness from your perceptions of smallness and helplessness to see through the lies that the ego protests are true. You remain enamoured of the ego's lies because they are still attractive to you. You believe them because you want to believe them. No one is forcing you at any time.

Until you own the attraction that judgement holds for you, you will delude yourself into thinking you have no other option than to judge. But judgement is unwise. It does not give rise to peace. Peace is not something for which you must struggle. It is not something you must earn. It is your birthright. It is always present in the depths of your being. To find it, do not seek outside yourself. No external situation can bring you peace if you do not want to be at peace. You must want peace with every part of your being. You must *want* to give up judgements and victimhood. You must *want* to recognise the Oneness of all life. And you must *want* to stop, rest in the stillness within, and savour the serenity that is ever at the depths of your soul.

You must want the truth so much that you will not tolerate within yourself any inclination to project judgement and blame. You must want deep peace with such longing that you will not heed the ego's seductive protestations of exploitation, persecution and maltreatment. You must see through the mask of self-righteousness the ego wears. You must be willing to acknowledge that you are responsible for all you experience and not listen to the ego's justifications for self-defence or its demands for retaliation. When you want Peace above all else, you will no longer be deceived by illusions.

If you want to see a world at peace, you must be at peace with what is. Allow the world to be just the way it is, and perhaps you will grow to love it as it is. It does not serve you to fight against the circumstances that manifest before you or argue against them. You do not need to hide from the world you see or indeed defend the world from criticism. Allow all to be just as it is and feel the peace that this acceptance brings you.

You have reached a point of no return. Now you cannot be consistently misled by the ego's false perceptions. The ego may continue using fear to entrap you, to convince you that there is something still to mistrust, something that warrants anxiety and self-defence. It will endeavour to distract you from living as the Christ that you are. Do not blindly walk away from your Self and enter the ego's dramas. Desire the Peace of God with such intensity that you will not allow yourself to be caught up in the ego's tales of woe.

The ego will continue to encourage you to find something wrong, but there is nothing wrong. It will continue to declare that you are separate from your Reality, but you know this is not so. You are ever One with the Father. Therefore, when the ego declares that you have cause to be afraid, do not heed it. Do not believe the fearful thoughts that dance frantically through the mind. Claim your freedom and know that *all* is well.

Beloved children of God, you are sacred in the eyes of all of us who love you and know the Truth of who you are. You are God Incarnate. This is not cause for boasting, but for humility. The Father sees no separation between all aspects of Himself. All expressions of the Father's Love are equal in every way. You are equal to me, and we are equal to the simplest, poorest soul who walked this planet. Similarly, we are equal to the richest, most powerful souls who govern the lives of others. Set no one above or below you, for the Father's Will declares that all are One. This demeans no one but raises all to the heights of Heaven.

Love all as your equal in every way, irrespective of education, wealth, talents, capability or standing in the community. The greatest saint is no more than the greatest sinner. All are equal expressions of the Father's Love. No one is better than you or more worthy, and

Chapter 17: Freedom from Illusion

no one is less than you. Love each one equally with the power of the Love that is within you. Love freely, no matter how or if that love is returned to you.

There are no accidental meetings. When you greet a brother or sister, remember that the encounter is holy, because you are holy. Every meeting is a sacred opportunity to share the Love that you are. Exempt no one from the radiance of your Love. If you do, you cast a shadow over the whole of creation. Past grievances can be healed in the presence of Love, and surely there is no greater gift to offer to the world than the healing of past discord. When the past is undone, this moment will shine forth in all the glory that is the Presence of God expressed in form. Love, then, your brothers and sisters with all your heart and all your soul and all your mind. If you would love the Father, then love His children. Let no shadow fall upon your world. Let no veils obscure the truth that radiates as the Son of God expressing the great Love and Beauty and Purity that God is.

The Earth is constantly undergoing change, but the spiritual essence of Mother Earth will endure forever. All life as you know it will come to an end because all things born into the realm of time will die. This death of form is not to be feared, for it but represents a transition. It does not mean the extinction of consciousness. All those creatures who have become extinct have completed their sojourn on Earth and are not to be lamented. Do not wish for their return. Their time here is over and will be no more. In time new species will appear, and the cycle will go on. Do not struggle to save those who have come to the end of their earthly visit but bring your love and your strength to restore peace to this planet. You do this by first restoring it to your own heart and mind.

The peace of the New Earth will not be established by efforting but by the power of Love. Love will heal the open wounds. It will cleanse the air and calm the waters. It will cool the fires of rebellion and soothe disturbed tempers. But do not ask it to bring back the past. This moment now is not to be tainted by what has been. This moment is free and new and alive with potential. Appreciate what it has to offer you, and do not look behind. And dwell not on the future, because if you do, you will lose sight of the beauty and holiness of what is available to you right now.

Each creation is unique and will follow its own path. You cannot judge the value of another soul's journey. You cannot perceive what is to be gained by all that another experiences and endures. Do not set out to 'fix' or 'save'. Come home to your Self and project no discrepancies onto others. Allow each one to walk their chosen road through this dream world. Do not fear for them but honour their choices. All souls will be called home to Heaven. The Holy Spirit knows how best to guide the soul's journey. If Love prompts you to speak or act, then do so, but be sure that it is the heart that is directing you and not the egoic mind. Only Love knows what best serves each soul. Only Love knows the mystery of Divinity that is at work in the lives of all God's children.

Come then unburdened unto the Father. Carry no cares, no concern for yourself or your world. Abandon all mistrust and uncertainty. Enter the Light free of weariness and hopelessness. Come home to God lightly, joyously and playfully. You can walk in this world and be not of it. You can abide on this planet without attachment to anyone or anything. You can step lightly through your days without fear in any form, without judgement and without guilt. You can be the presence of Peace, and a Light that shines away the darkness.

The journey home is a journey that takes you over high mountains and through deep chasms, through moments of great glory and moments of profound sorrow. And as you draw near the end of the trail, you look back with wonder at all you have experienced: all the dramas, all the joys, all the suffering and all the exhilaration.

Chapter 17: Freedom from Illusion

What does it all mean? Does it mean anything at all? Is it not just all experience, experience you have freely chosen? Even though you have lost sight of who you really are, you experienced only what you wanted to experience.

You are not the small fear-driven one you have believed yourself to be. You are limitless, infinite and eternal. You are divine. As you look back on the roads you have travelled, be grateful for every step you have taken. Look upon your fear and laugh, for it calls for laughter. And if fear yet remains in your consciousness, befriend it. Take its arm and let it walk at your side as you take the next step. If you befriend it, it will provide you with gifts that support your journey. Only as you ignore it, hide from it, deny it, or push it away from you, will it cling to you more desperately, and rob you of Peace.

Fear is not your enemy – not now, not ever. But you have feared the fear, and made it seem much larger and more threatening than it really is. In Reality it has no substance. It is just a movement of energy, a thought in your mind. You have viewed it through a veil of deception and given it characteristics that have darkened your awareness. As you are about to take the next step in your journey, be aware that fear has much to teach you.

When you take the arm of fear and allow it to be present beside you as you walk, you can become aware that Peace is present also. As you stride out without resisting anything, you will recognise that underneath your trembling, there is a calmness and strength that is more real than the fear. And there will come a time when this much-maligned companion is no longer with you. He has quietly fallen behind you. You have no need of his companionship now. He has taught you all he can. So, you walk quietly and contentedly forward on your way, and the awareness of Love is present within you. You are free.

Your Infinite Potential

The time has come to fully embrace your Reality as Christ, to know there is only One and you are that One. This requires that you banish all self-judgement from your awareness and come to love your Self as the expression of Love in form. Self-judgement is born of a lie, a misconception that you are separate and alone. You have believed yourself to be small, weak and insignificant. But you are Christ, and because it is the Father who lives and breathes through you, you are powerful beyond the conception of the small mind that has been ruling your awareness.

Your potential is infinite. It is infinite because the mind is infinite. Your mind knows no boundaries. You have only to have faith in your vision. You have the power to perform miracles. You too can heal. You too can quieten the storm. You too can multiply the loaves and the fishes. You must believe it is possible. You cannot in Truth limit the Son of God. How can you impose limits on what is limitless? How can you confine within the realms of time that which is timeless? You are only limited by your beliefs.

While you cling to outmoded notions of limitation and insignificance, of weakness and fear, you will not break free from the prison of your delusions about who you are and what you can do. You are free, and you are infinite and eternal. You are powerful and loving. No concepts can hold you prisoner except by your own agreement. You hold the key to liberate yourself. This key lies not outside of you but in the depths of your mind.

Always remember the Truth of who you are. What does this mean? It means that in every situation that arises, from whatever perspective you glimpse your world, you can remember your power and the presence of God within you. What is fear but a creation of mind? What is worry but an expectation of what is to come, coloured by misinterpretations. All is well always. Break down the walls of the self-concept you hold. You are not the personality, you are not the body, you are not walking about the planet breathing air. This is not you, although this is what you seem to be. This is only because you have this habit of focusing your awareness within the body. You seem to be looking out through those eyes, touching objects with those hands, hearing with those ears. But you are none of these things. You are pure consciousness, and you are divine.

When you withdraw your attention from the body, you can become aware that you are simply watching a series of events that seem to progress forward into the future. This series of events seems to be happening to an individual, a human being on a planet that is spinning around the sun which is but one star amidst a galaxy of stars. In the infinity of the universe, you seem to be a small mass of cells and organs within the confines of a body living a life in a limited arena, performing your tasks, sleeping, eating, gathering with friends and family. But this is not who you are. You are the enormity of it, the greatness of it all. If you can begin to watch this movie on which you are focused, and begin to realise it is just a movie, you can begin to taste freedom. If you can begin to liberate yourself from the concepts and beliefs, the thoughts and emotions that stream through the mind, they will not confine you any longer.

You have misunderstood the nature of your world. You think it is solid and subject to certain natural laws. You think it will endure through time, changing little. But your world is changing

Chapter 18: Your Infinite Potential

dramatically. It is not solid, nor bound by the laws you believe to govern it. The Earth is an expression of the Father's Love. It is energy. It is intelligence and it is consciousness. What you see is not real because you are seeing only images constructed in the mind based on pre-conceived ideas. You believe that what you see is reality. You see merely your own projections and will continue to do so until you stop projecting your beliefs outwards.

I have asked that you relinquish *all* your beliefs. And why is this so? Because your beliefs are based on the false concept of separation. You have believed yourself to be a body because you see yourself as an individual entity apart from your brothers and sisters. But remember, you are not a body, nor ever have been. You have constructed this whole world of seemingly separate bodies that are born onto this planet, live out their lifespan and then die. The body appears to sicken and age as the years pass, and so you have come to fear growing old. You experience the body aging because you believe in ageing. It is deeply entrenched in your mind. Death too is an illusion. Because you believe in death, it has become your greatest fear. You fear extinction. But you will never die and need not fear what is not real.

Your potential is infinite, but your beliefs limit you and cripple you. Perhaps you have a belief that people should be kind and considerate? That the innocent should be protected? That children should be cared for? That it is wrong to hurt or steal from another? That offenders should pay for their crimes? I suggest that you write out your own list. How many 'shoulds' do you have? Look honestly upon your thoughts and reactions and determine what beliefs you are holding. How many expectations do you hold about your own behaviour? Each 'should' reflects the belief that the world must function according to rules that you have established in your mind. But what happens when these rules are ignored or broken? How do you react? Do you not become defensive and lose your sense of peace? Does the body not become tense and constricted?

Do you question this and feel we need to be compassionate? Does not compassion demand that others be kind? Does not compassion call for the innocent to be protected and children cared for? Observe how you define compassion. As pity or empathy? Does it call for the rescue of others or the correction of a problem? Remember that all have called to themselves whatever they experience. There are no accidents. If you feel compelled to rescue or fix, remember that you are not asked to change the dream but change your mind about it. Love does not deny the dream but sees beyond the dream into the essence of the Truth of all.

Love is ever compassionate. Love always loves. And Love is always in allowance. To love is to accept what is. To experience any form of resistance to the events playing out before you is to experience a loss of peace. Because only Love is real, if you see other than Love, know you look upon illusion. Love does not see victims. It does not judge. It does not assume. It does not protest. It simply loves.

Look about you with wonder, not with consternation. Look upon all with eyes of love, not judgement. If you have a rigid belief that 'others should be kind' and insist they act according to your expectations, are you not playing the dictator? Allow them to act according to their own dictates. Remember you are always seeing that which you project outwards. If you perceive another acting with unkindness, ask 'Where have I been unkind?' When you believe others should be kind, are you not also failing to confront unkindness in yourself? If you perceive something occurring that you believe requires action, you need only go within and ask for the guidance of the Comforter.

To maintain your peace of mind, all beliefs must be renounced. There is nothing wrong and this world does not need to be run according to your rules and expectations. You are not asked to

Chapter 18: Your Infinite Potential

judge and control the behaviour of others, but to allow all to be as it is. There is nothing wrong because all events are neutral. What is taking place is a divine orchestration. Love is acting upon the hearts and minds of God's children. Look upon every occurrence as an expression of Love or a call for Love. Every occurrence presents an opportunity to open and to extend Love to all.

So, it is time to finally and completely let go – to let go of all beliefs, all 'certainties', of the sense of need, of all attachment to emotional states. All must be shed. The time of your awakening is at hand. All that is required is a relinquishment, not a striving or a seeking. Just finally renouncing all control, surrendering unto the Will of the Father. It is a relaxing, a softening, a letting go of all you have held dear and clung to for security. What need have you for security when you are already secure? You are everything. You are whole. You are enough.

The path to self-realisation is not paved by illusory concepts. It is paved by Love. Each paving stone is hewn out of the rock of Truth by the hands committed to self-honesty and self-awareness. You cannot follow this path into the Kingdom of Heaven bearing the burdens of your old attitudes and beliefs. You must be willing to cast them from you as useless and cumbersome. Toss aside all belief in fear and separation. Cast aside all perception of lack, all concept of limitation, all judgements and defensive reactions. You do not need them. They will not serve you. Only Love will serve you now.

Step out on this path confidently, with lightness of step, liberated from your ancient burdens. Without the weight of your judgements and expectations, you will walk freely and joyously towards your goal. No longer will you feel small and limited or be restrained by fear. Nor will the concept of separation blind you to the Oneness of all life. Your heart will rejoice because you have been freed from the prison you constructed. You see clearly now because the Father's Love is illuminating the path before you. Glad of heart, you eagerly anticipate the glory of the Kingdom of God that awaits you. Now the Light of Love is radiating from within you, and you see it reflected in all that you look upon. You recognise it as your true Self. Now you have entered the Kingdom and can begin your journey within it. All illusions of separation have dissolved and there is only One.

The Wisdom of the Body

Many times, we have told you that this world is a figment of the imagination, a dream world, a sacred experiment in experiencing the illusion of separation. Never need you fear anything. Never need you fear for the body. If the body should become ill or injured, you need never worry or fret about its condition. Do not judge the body, no matter what it manifests. Do not judge yourself for what the body experiences. We have told you again and again that you are not the body. You are a wondrous creation of Love, of joy and of divinity. You are the offspring of the Father. You are Love Itself.

It does not matter in the world of dreams what the body demonstrates. *It does not matter*. You take the body too seriously. You think you should manifest the perfect body and fret when it is ill or diseased. Have I not told you that only the ego suffers? Anything you experience in the body is just an experience. It is not wrong. It does not have to be corrected. You need change nothing. When you judge the body, you do not know what you do. The energy of judgement will always be limiting.

Love the body as it is. What does it matter in Truth if it is deformed or injured, overweight or underweight, diseased or scarred? *It does not matter*. It is just an experience that you have drawn to yourself – to experience it. If you were to climb a steep and rugged mountain, you might arrive at the summit and exclaim at the view. Why do you do this? Is not the journey as equally significant as the arrival at the summit? Do not discount the journey. Bring a sense of wonder to every moment you experience.

When you are experiencing an illness, a misshapen body, or a body damaged by what you presume to be an accident, how will you respond? We have spoken to you before of the power of the mind and how you can use it to change your circumstances in this world. You can use it to fight an enemy or hug a friend. You can use it to create abundance or a beautiful score of music. You can use it to punish yourself or cherish yourself. This is your choice. Never are you a victim of anything.

Now hear me well. Healing is always of the mind. It is the mind that governs the condition of the body. To heal the body, the mind must be healed. And of what must the mind be healed? Of all thought of fear. It is fear in its many forms that leads to disharmony and ill health in the body. Hatred causes the cells to constrict and malfunction. Anger provokes the secretion of substances within the cells that promotes degeneration. And when fear engulfs the mind, it can seem as though the body has turned against itself. Does this mean that the wisdom and intelligence of the body are not present? Indeed not. It has merely been over-ridden by the emotions that have gripped the mind.

When the mind is at peace, when harmony has been restored, this great wisdom that is Love will restore order to the body and bring peace and health to the cells. When your mind is calm and centred in Love, you give no heed to the body. And yet it continues to function unaided, without any conscious control by your mind. What allows this to happen? It is Love itself, alive in each of the cells that enables them to resume the roles they were created to fulfil. At any one moment a multitude of actions is occurring within the body, allowing it to breathe and move about upon the planet. Thus, Love can use it as a means to support the purposes of the atonement.

Chapter 19: The Wisdom of the Body

So true healing is an act of love. If you ingest some medication in fear of illness, can it bring about a true healing? If the symptoms are temporarily alleviated, does this mean a true healing has taken place? Indeed not. Do not be convinced that an apparent improvement in the health of the body is evidence of true healing. True healing is always of the mind. Why is this so? Because you are not the body. You are spirit, infinite and eternal, created in the image of your Father.

Because you are One with all that is, you never make a choice in isolation. The Will of God is always an expression of Love. It is always an extension of Love. You do not stand alone at any time. You are an intricate part of the whole and are moved by forces and energies beyond your comprehension. Illness can be a great gift, not something to frown upon. Cease to judge the body for what it manifests. Honour it, cleanse it, feed it nourishing foods, clothe it in beautiful costumes, shelter it from storms. But remember that it belongs not to you. It belongs to God. If you would surrender to the Will of the Father, can you not also relinquish the fate of the body unto Him?

When you do so you will know you need have no concern about what the body experiences. If it should experience paralysis or severe wounds, do not judge this as bad or wrong, or something for which to grieve. Your experience with the body is temporary. Your soul is eternal and ever free. Beloveds, relinquish all fear. If you could but trust all that happens, you would understand that everything is in your best interests. *Everything.*

So then, how do you care for the body? Do you exercise it? Do you adopt a special diet? Do you feed it vitamins and minerals? Do you practise fasting? We say to you: what does your heart say? What does Love ask of you? Do nothing out of fear. Question why you adopt the diets you follow. Question why you take the supplements you ingest. Question what you fear when you desperately seek outside of yourself for solutions to the pain you experience. Pain is always an expression of resistance. When you learn to listen deeply to your pain and open to hear the voice of Truth it speaks, you will understand that it comes laden with gifts. Never equate pain with suffering, for have we not told you often enough that only the ego suffers.

Relinquish all your concerns to the Holy Spirit and trust all that unfolds in your life in this dream world. Practise allowance continually. Do not judge what lies beyond your jurisdiction. Honour the body, yes, but remember that it belongs not to you. Let Love use the body for its own purposes, purposes that the small self cannot comprehend. Trust what is unfolding in the body and love it for *all* it manifests.

You need have no fear for the body or its demise. You are not the body, and though the body has no reality, the Love that gives it life is real. It is real because it emanates from the Father. Love abides in all that you see because Love is in your mind. Honour the body, not as something outside of you but as an expression of Love in form. Nurture it and love it. In caring for it, you demonstrate love for your Self.

What if the body becomes ill? When the tissues become diseased or manifest an imbalance, know that this is an opportunity for you to go within and listen to the message the body is communicating. When the body is unwell, it is not your enemy. Its essence is ever the Love that the Father is. It is simply informing you that in some way the mind is out of balance. The body always out-pictures the thoughts in the mind.

If you are feeling burdened or are suppressing sadness, the body will elicit symptoms of tiredness and heaviness. If a part of the body is numb, ask yourself - 'Where am I numbing my mind or emotions?' If the body is feeling stiff or rigid, ask – 'Am I displaying rigidity in my attitudes and beliefs?' If you are experiencing pain, ask –

Chapter 19: The Wisdom of the Body

'Why do I believe punishment is justified?' Whatever understanding is being offered to you by the body's symptoms, you can choose to heed the message that you have been given. Never are you a victim of them. The body is a projection of the mind, and manifests only what is birthed in the mind.

I have advised you not to attempt to change the world but to be willing to change your thoughts about it. When the body falls ill, do you not desire to heal it? If you experience pain, do you not reach for a tablet to alleviate it? If your eyesight is impaired, do you not don spectacles to enable the physical eyes to see clearly? If a bone in the arm is broken, do you not seek to have it reset? This is not wrong. You are free to choose how you will respond to all that you experience. Tension, disease and broken bones are a manifestation of some form of fear, and it is helpful to minimise the fear in ways that seem appropriate. But remember that the seeds of the symptoms lie in the mind. The real cause of your pain and discomfort is always in the mind.

Fear can blind you to the truth but trust not the fear. When you have alleviated the symptoms, you can then address the real cause that lies in the mind. Go beyond the fear and choose to abide in Love. Love accepts all things, trusts in all that eventuates, and thus can transcend all things. Allow yourself to be present with the pain or discomfort in whatever form it takes. Relax and let go of your tension and resistance. Allow things to be just as they are. If fear arises, do not run from it or deny it. Allow it to be. Feel it. Relax into the pain. Do not resist it. Simply allow it to be what it is. Allow all that it has been masking to come into your awareness. Allow all the suppressed emotions to be felt, all fearful attitudes to be questioned and all false beliefs to be discerned. This is the path of healing. This is the path that heeds and honours the body and uplifts the soul.

When you finally relinquish the need to control the circumstances of your life, you will recognise the significance of your motivations.

When you accept that everything is in your best interests, you will be less willing to judge what manifests in your own body or the body of another. Many times we have called on you to allow and allow and allow. You are not the director of your life. Your thoughts have power in the world of dreams, but you are not alone. You are one with all that is, one with the great beauty and mystery that is God. If you would honour the Will of the Father, question your motivations and trust what unfolds in your life. And trust in the power of Love to work miracles.

When you experience pain, it will only seem overwhelming as you resist it. If you can surrender to it fully, you will not need to deny the pain, shrink from it, hate it, withdraw from it, fight it, flee from it, or resist it in any way. You can simply allow it to arise in your awareness and feel it, loving yourself as you do so. It is your very resistance to it that makes it seem so huge and dark and overwhelming.

So, is pain necessary? Can pain be minimised? Is suffering inevitable? We remind you again: only the ego suffers. Pain is not necessary but if *you* have decided to experience it – consciously or unconsciously – you will experience it. But it will have a message for you. It will teach you something about yourself. It will show you what you have fought against and resisted. Does this mean that if you or another are experiencing pain or illness that you should not use the power of mind to support the healing of the body? You have been granted free will but be wise in how you use it. Can you truly know what the Will of God is in all situations of illness or injury? Can you know who will benefit as events unfold? Can you be sure that it is not in the best interests of all concerned that the body becomes ill or does not survive?

We have frequently advised you to relinquish judgement. We have told you that you do not truly know what anything is or is for. Can you begin to trust what is and simply allow all things to

Chapter 19: The Wisdom of the Body

be as they are? And love them as they are? Remember that you need do nothing. Does this mean that you should not take some action? Indeed not. You *need* do nothing, but you can respond to any situation with love or without love, with love or with fear. It is your choice. Only when you trust in the power of Love and let it guide your every moment will you know peace and the certainty of divine fulfilment. Only when you trust what is, just as it is, will you know the wisdom of allowance. Only then will you know God.

There is nothing that is outside of you. The universe is infinite, and yet smaller than a grain of sand. Just as you are a thought in the Mind of God, so is the universe a thought in the mind of God's Son. The universe is infinite because your mind is infinite. There are no limits to your consciousness. You are eternal. You are everything. There is only One – One Creation, One Life, One God – and you are that One. When the realisation dawns upon you that you are One with all that is, you will begin to sense the great mystery that penetrates the world because God Is. All is God and there is nothing apart from God.

The Breath of Life

Beloved friends, these words come to you from the depths of who you are, where we are joined as One. Separation is a lie. You are the Holy Child of God, and you are part of my Self. You are a star: not such a star as waxes and wanes in the night sky, but one that shines brightly eternally. Your essence is Love. Nothing you think, nothing you believe, can diminish your light. Be that which you are now and shine your light upon the world. Be in the world but not of the world. You have only to let go, relax and trust, and simply allow all things to be as they are.

We speak to you now of the nature of the breath. Breath is the very thing that gives the body life. When breathing ceases, the body will cease to be, even as the Truth of who you are continues into new worlds and new experiences. There is only Love, and because the essence of the air you breathe is Love, the breath of life is the breath of God. When you inhale, you are breathing in Love. When the air is expelled, you are sending out Love into the world. Feel the sweetness present in the very air you breathe.

Be mindful of your breathing now. Is the breath shallow or deep? Is the breathing rapid or slow? Appreciate how the breath is sustaining the life of the body. Rest in the silence and become aware of your breath. Not as a mechanism that allows the body to function, but as the precious gift that it is. Feel the air moving deeply into the abdomen. Do not seek to control it. Allow it to move as the body wills. Simply sit quietly and watch as the chest rises and falls, unhindered by any agendas. As you do this, you will become conscious that it seems to have a life and intelligence of its own. Trust this and let it carry you more deeply within yourself.

Each time you inhale, feel yourself sinking even more profoundly into the silence. Sense the great depth of peace awaiting you here. Feel the richness of the Love that dwells here and the profound stillness within the silence that lies here awaiting your discovery. As you are carried more deeply within, feel each breath leading you into the very presence of God. And here you can rest, simply rest, doing nothing, seeking nothing. Simply rest. For what greater joy can you discover apart from this? Here there is no disharmony. Here there is no striving. Here there is no discord. Here is only the presence of Love.

As you abide in this deep place of silence, know that I rest here with you. As you feel the presence of the One who has birthed you, know that I too was birthed by this One and live in the sweetness of His Presence. You and I are ever One with the Father. We are never apart from Him. When you became lost in the dream of separation, you lost sight of that which is real. Now your breath can become the means that enables you to descend into the depths of your being, into the presence of God. Here you can realise the Truth of who you are – not a body moving through time and space, but pure spirit, the essence of Love. I will meet you here. Together we will rest in the silence of the Heart we share as One and know the peace that is beyond all understanding.

Precious friends, peace is your rightful inheritance. It is not to be found outside of you. It resides always in the depths of your being. It can be realised any time you choose to enter the portal of the breath and enter the silence therein. Do this regularly and abide with me in the quietness that proffers you that depth of peace that is

Chapter 20: The Breath of Life

the only offering that will satisfy the yearning of your soul. You are kin to me. We are of one lineage. I am your brother and your friend, and because you are not apart from me, we can know the joy and sweetness of joining as One in this place of silence. Let, then, the breath carry you here often, that we may come together and rest in the great depths of peace that the Father has gifted to us.

Know that your quiet breathing can be used to demolish obstacles to the presence of Love. When you experience the vagaries of the ego, you meet with judgement, blame, guilt and suffering, manipulation and control. The ego justifies a defensive response because it assumes it knows what others are thinking and what motivates them. It believes it is not safe until it can find protection from what is 'out there'. This illusion leads to suffering and a loss of peace.

When you bring awareness to your breathing, this will return you to the present moment and shift the mind away from the delusions of the ego. Breathe deeply and feel the quietness this brings to the mind. Now you have created space between the mad thoughts of self-defence and can recall the wisdom of forgiveness. Now you can begin to question the truth of your painful thoughts and remember that only Love is real. Each breath will progressively relax the body and dissolve the tension in the nervous system. Clarity of mind can expose the insanity of the ego's thought system. With the restoration of peace, you can see clearly that all is well, and that the event that occurred was simply a lesson in love.

Sustained breathing can assist you to release the old emotions long held in the body that limit its health and hinder your maturation as a soul. Deep and rhythmic breath can become an open channel for painful memories to arise and suppressed emotions to be felt and released. You need only lie quietly in a comfortable position and breathe slowly and deeply. As you continue to practise deep rhythmical breathing, oxygen will flood the cells. You may experience tingling in the tissues of the body, feelings of tiredness or other unusual sensations. Trust this and continue to breathe.

If you do not resist what arises, you may become aware of strong emotions. If you become conscious of fear, know that it is fear from the past, and needs only to be felt to be released. If anger arises, do not judge it or restrict its progress. Simply feel it. If sadness arises, honour the emotion and let the tears flow if they emerge. Keep breathing, deeply and rhythmically. Let the air move deeply into the abdomen and feel the chest expand as the lungs fill with this precious air. Oxygen becomes your gift to the cells of the body, allowing them to release the emotional tensions long held within them. When you feel a sense of completion, lie still at peace, and let the breath grow quieter. Rest in gratitude for all you have experienced. If you feel the need for support during this process, ask another to be with you. Ensure that the one who offers to share this time with you as you breathe is strong in wisdom and has released enough of their own pain to be fully present with you.

If you commit to this process, it will serve you in ways that you cannot now imagine. It will release ancient tensions from the body and old painful memories from your mind. You may recall memories of other lives and other eras. Do not dwell on these. Let them arise in your consciousness, feel what needs to be felt, see what needs to be seen, and let them go. Give the past back to the past and do not glorify it. Then bring your awareness back to this time, this moment, this body and the environment in which you abide now. Thus, this act of breathing can become a precious gift to release you from the past, that you may be restored fully into the present moment.

As you value the movement of breath that gives the body life, value the great gift that your life is. Your life is precious. This Earth is precious. Your brothers and sisters are precious. All is a wondrous expression of the Father's Love. Now a new world is being birthed. You can choose to relinquish all the old attitudes and behaviours

Chapter 20: The Breath of Life

exhibited by the ego and claim your Christhood. You can honour the gift of your life and use it to use time differently, to embrace the truth that only Love is real, and only Love will lead you into the new world. You can use the power of your breath to heal and support your awakening from the dream of separation.

Only you can make this choice for yourself. You have but to choose Love over fear. You need but recognise the insanity of the ego's perceptions to see that it is the only logical choice to make. Use the power of your mind to set yourself free and make the decision to see the Oneness that is the reality before you. We love you, and we await your awakening. Do not to delay – wait no longer to decide for Love. Why stay asleep in a dreamworld when the Father is beckoning you home? When you finally make the choice for Love, you will enter the Kingdom of Heaven and begin your journey within it.

The Illusion of Time

The moment has come for you to step off the path leading you aimlessly through this dream world. Follow the path that is paved with Love. This will usher you towards inner peace and trust and lead you on to allowance and surrender. Signposts will direct you in the right direction, signposts designated: forgiveness, sinlessness, honesty, gentleness, openness, playfulness and joy. Each signpost is both a guide, and a confirmation that you are awakening from the dream. The path may at times be rough beneath your feet, and it may seem to twist and turn in unexpected ways, but always it is leading you onwards towards the Truth. As each signpost is passed, your heart will feel lighter. Now you can feel the Grace of God descending upon you.

If you travel the path contentedly, you will know that there is nothing to fear and great reason to celebrate. Those lost in the darkness of illusion will look upon you with wonder. They will question the wisdom of your choices but will recognise the peace that reigns in your heart. If you step out confidently, undistracted by any dramas you see played out around you, fear will not cloud your awareness. Love has awakened within you. Those who look upon you with gratification will find comfort in your presence. Your quiet assurance that all is well will speak louder than all the ego's protestations of fear. The Son of God is yearning for his home now.

Hear the call of Love, and doubt not the wisdom of its message. Fear would lead you deeper into the darkness, but Love will hold your hand and guide you safely home.

In Truth you are home now, but until you awaken to the realisation that the separation never occurred, you will still believe in the illusion of time and think there is yet some distance to travel. Time was birthed when the idea of separation entered the mind of the Son, and in that moment a world was created, a world of planets and stars, and universe upon universe. This world of time has brought you to this moment now, and you have the opportunity now to awaken from the dream and embrace your reality as Christ.

Your concept of time is a misperception. You have believed time to be sequential and linear. Do not your clocks tell you so? But your clocks deceive you. Time is an illusion created by the ego to justify judgement and condemnation. There is no past and no future. You believe that cause and effect are separated by moments of time, but there is *only* now. Each moment you experience is a new beginning. In Truth it does not arise in the past, nor cause an effect in the future. Cause and effect are concurrent.

Such is the power of your beliefs, however, that you are convinced that what has occurred in the past affects what you experience now. In Reality nothing is occurring. Your world, and all you experience, is imagined. In Reality there is only the Light of God shining forth in all its glory. However, because you believe in time, you bring the past with you into the present and feel that you have reason to fear the future. You then believe guilt and worry are warranted. The concept of time deludes the egoic mind into thinking that a brother's error yesterday justifies your condemnation of him today. You feel your feelings of hurt and victimhood are vindicated, and you rescind your responsibility for your own emotional responses. It is only because your mind continues to recreate the sense of victimisation that you can experience it now.

Chapter 21: The Illusion of Time

If you accept that time is unreal, you can no longer sustain resentment and victimhood. When can you find peace except by choosing it now? When can you extend Love if not now? And when can you wake up, if not now? Now is the only time to awaken. Let go of your conviction that you can awaken from the dream sometime in the future. There is no future. This belief only serves to delay your decision, to avoid awakening to the Truth right now.

Your belief that time is real has enabled you to manifest a dreamworld that progresses forward hour by hour, day by day. You read a book from the first page to the last. Your cars record the kilometres travelled over time. In numerous ways your belief in time is reinforced, but it remains a false belief. You are always responsible for what you experience. Your thoughts have given rise to the world you perceive – the meetings, the surroundings, the events – and to the illusion of time. Because you created time, you can become free of the limitations it imposes by recognising its unreality.

Nowhere are you taught that you must confine yourself within the parameters of time. Yet you do this freely, by your own choice. You can choose anew. Time governs the pattern of your days. You watch the hands of the clock and believe that you must perform tasks at specific times. You set your clocks to arise at a certain time. You eat your meals at certain times. You rush to be at your workplace at a certain time. If you are late, feelings of frustration and tension arise, and peace eludes you. But even if you are stuck in a traffic jam and late for an appointment, you can choose to trust what is arising in the moment. You can remember that you are wholly responsible for your experience and make the decision for peace.

Because you believe in time and carry the past into the present, you do not see anything as it really is. You see only the past. When you look upon a brother, you do not recognise him. You see only a bundle of impressions that you have held onto from the past.

You view him through the veil of all the previous judgements and perceptions you have held about him. Because you have projected your own opinions, fears and insecurities onto him, you fail to see the Reality of his being. When you look upon a tree, your previous encounters with trees are recalled and obscure your perception of the beautiful creation before you. The very act of labelling imposes limitations on what you are seeing. By labelling a form a 'tree', your recollection of other trees causes you to compartmentalise the creation before you. You do not see it as it is. You do not see it as a perfect expression of God in form.

Brothers and sisters, be fully present in this moment now. There are no ordinary moments because each is filled with extraordinary potential. Each moment is precious. Each moment is a new beginning. Each is offering you the opportunity to relinquish all judgement and blame and choose Love over fear. Each holds the promise of peace. If you could renounce all belief in time, you would see the glory of the real world shining in the light of the Father's Love. All is Love. All is Light. When time is dissolved, only this vision will remain. Before time was, I AM. When time is no more, I AM. You are eternal. All concept of birth and death is illusory. What arises in time, ends in time, but you are changeless. You remain as you always are, the only begotten Son of God.

When you have seen the unreality of time, guilt will have no meaning. Trust not those who speak of man's guilt and declare that he is being punished by a wrathful God because he has sinned. Man has not sinned, and he warrants no guilt. Sin is impossible because your Father has created you in His image. You are the wondrous expression of Love in form, and free to create on the canvas of your mind whatever you will. Your Father knows only Love and sees only the Truth of who you are. Now you can choose to paint a world of love, a world of great beauty and happiness. If you choose Love, it will find its rightful home in your mind, and it will wield the brush

Chapter 21: The Illusion of Time

that builds a new world that reveals the Truth that only Love is real.

Time is misunderstood, but the egoic mind is unable to understand what is beyond its abilities. Do not judge yourself if you yet struggle to comprehend the illusion that time is. The ego will defend itself against anything that threatens its existence. While you continue to believe you are a body, you will be reluctant to abandon the belief in time. This belief has formed the structure of your days, and if you accept that time is an illusion, your long-held beliefs will be challenged. You are waking up by degrees as fear loosens its hold on your mind, and as fear retreats, your old beliefs will be relinquished. Be content to acknowledge time's illusory nature. If you do not fully understand this now, we remind you that there is nothing in Truth that you need to understand. Simply know that only Love is real and relax, let go and let all things be as they are. Own your divinity and shine your light upon the world.

In the Quiet of the Forest

Healing comes to a soul in many forms, and by many avenues. The depth of healing is determined by the soul's willingness to open and perceive all that has been hidden from the conscious mind, and to forgive. Forgiveness requires that the soul acknowledge its full responsibility for everything that is experienced. Often have we reminded you that there are no accidents, and you can never be a victim of what you see. Always you remain the sovereign master of your life.

There is never any justification for judgement of yourself or another, for all events are neutral and the Power of God lies within you as your true Self. Always are you free, and you owe no obligation to any other soul. Your only task is to fulfil the Father's Will, and this is not an obligation but a choice. Ever do you remain as you were created to be, the essence of Love in form. You are the offspring of the Father, and time and space do not limit you.

These words that you read seem to come to you from a source outside of you, but this is not so. These words arise in your awareness because they are *your* words and have arisen before you to remind you of what you already know. These words are not foreign to you but appear on this page now because you have chosen to awaken and realise the Truth of your being. Too long have you remained lost in the illusion of separation. Too long have you believed yourself to be something other than what you are. Too long have you been imprisoned by concepts that have no place in the mind of the one who would know God.

My brothers and sisters, come home now to the Kingdom of Heaven, come home to your Self. In truth this is where you have always been, but you lost sight of this in your exploration of all that God is not. Because only Love is real, and because God is but Love, you can find your Self again by relinquishing fear and embracing the Love that you are. Be mindful that this is not a difficult thing to do. How could you believe that this is difficult when you realise that this knowledge of who you truly are is present within you now and always?

You have only to brush from your eyes the cobwebs of illusion that have obscured your vision. Cobwebs have little substance and can be swept away with a simple movement of the hand. But while you continue to believe that these cobwebs are a firm obstruction to your vision, you will remain imprisoned by this belief.

Your habit of believing your thoughts has confused you. Look objectively upon your thoughts and give them no power over you. Let not your beliefs control you but see them for what they are. And your beliefs are many. You share many beliefs with others and so have created the consensus thought forms that have shaped your world. Your beliefs are only concepts, concepts that you are convinced reflect reality. They are habitual thoughts you have believed to be true. But they do not reflect Reality.

You believe you are a body, and you believe in illness. You believe that judgement is justified, and blame is warranted. You believe that loss is possible, and that if you struggle hard enough, you can gain what you believe you lack. You have been convinced that such lies are true. But you are not a body, and only those who believe in the possibility of sickness can become ill. And judgement is never justified because it is not possible for a child of God to sin.

Chapter 22: In the Quiet of the Forest

All judgements are projections, because everything you see in this world of illusions is your projection. Loss is not possible, and you are already all you need to be.

Judgement is the anathema of this world. It distorts your perception and robs you of peace. The suffering you experience is created by your own mind. Let not the mind be your master, but delegate it the role of the obedient servant. Let it not rule you but allow it to become a willing helper that supports your journey and serves the Atonement.

Truth cannot be defiled, but it can be obscured. You may hide from it, but you cannot destroy it. You can deny it, but you cannot dispute it. For Truth shines forth eternally, untainted and undeterred by false beliefs or misconceptions. It does not require anything of you – no analysis, no interpretation, and no confirmation. Truth simply is. You have only to recognise it and embrace it.

Come with me now on a journey into the Light. Imagine for a time that you are standing at the edge of a great forest. Look up and about you at the grandeur of your brothers the trees and the gentle energy they emanate. Visualise your hand being raised and resting on the trunk of a tree. Feel the tree's presence. Sense the life force within it. Experience the welcoming shelter of the canopy of leaves above you. Perceive the delicacy of the rays of sunlight filtering through the leaves. Feel the Presence of God alive before you.

Now imagine you are stepping out deeper into the forest. Know that the busy world outside the forest has fallen away behind you. Feel the increasing coolness of the air as you walk deeper into this woodland. The soft carpet of fallen leaves beneath your feet muffles the sound of your footsteps, and the quietness of this glade caresses your soul. Here in this wonderland peace is present and is offering you its blessings.

Now you feel the presence not only of the individual trees themselves, but of the forest itself. It speaks to you in the stillness.

THE ASCENDENCE OF LOVE

It embraces you with the Love that is its essence. Stop, stand still, and *feel* the forest. What is it whispering to you? What is it asking of you? Feel the answer within you. Let not the thinking mind dominate your awareness now. Follow the vision in the mind and allow it to lead you onwards. Trust what it is offering to you, without rationalising what you are experiencing.

Visualise one of the ancient trees before you. See yourself lowering the body and sitting at its base. Lean back against its trunk and feel the texture of its bark beneath your clothing. Feel the power of its love supporting you. Rest there quietly, taking comfort in its presence, and feel stillness seeping into your soul. Be grateful for the Love it is extending to you in this moment of time. And as you rest in this quiet place, feel the reality of the peace that always lies within you. Let the movement of your breath carry you even deeper into the stillness, even deeper into a more intimate connection with this tree, this sacred life-form. What gentle response can you offer it for the gift of peace it has extended to you?

Be mindful now that you are never alone. At all times are you One with all Life. This tree is your brother and your friend and is ever One with you. You are not apart from the natural world. This journey into this forest is not some idle excursion into a fantasy world. I have brought you into this forest to remind you of the gifts of spirit that the natural world has to offer you. In your rush to achieve, in your determination to produce bigger and better, in your eagerness to expand and gain ever more, you have lost sight of your kinship with Nature. You have lost sight of the wonder and great beauty that lies beyond the busy world of man and his machines.

The bodies that you call your own were born out of the ground of Mother Earth. It is she who provides you with the food that you eat, the clothing you wear, and the materials for the homes that shelter you. You are not apart from her. She is essential to the life that you live, your wellbeing and your happiness. Yet she has felt the

Chapter 22: In the Quiet of the Forest

effects of your insane beliefs. You have shut out the natural world and separated from her. If you would restore the planet to health and harmony, awaken to the Truth of who you are and demonstrate to the world the Love and the Peace you wish to see reflected out in the world. Respect all life and live each day with Love as your guide and your only motivation.

Indeed, you are free to manifest what you will upon this planet. Nothing is wrong. We do not judge you. We do not condemn you for the choices you make and will always honour your decisions. But if you desire peace, if you wish to see the love and harmony of the New Earth evolve on this planet, it would be wise to re-establish your relationship with your Earth Mother.

It will be helpful to become more aware of the natural world and fully understand the effect of your decisions upon it. Do not fear that in doing so you will be deprived of what you need to thrive and be happy. There is nothing to fear. If you re-establish your bonds with Nature, you will lose nothing that has any intrinsic value, but this relationship will fulfil you and enrich your life. It is time to acknowledge the sacred presence of the natural world and return to Mother Earth the love that she has always held for her children. Observe the effects of your actions upon her forests and waterways, and the very air you breathe. What choices could you make now that will demonstrate love for Mother Earth and enhance the quality of life on this planet?

This is the question we ask you to address. No longer bury your head in the sand. This is a call to all who would be part of the healing of planet Earth, to all who would willingly follow the promptings of Love. To heal the planet, you do not need to go out and fight for her salvation. Love does not battle against supposed offenders. Love simply loves.

To heal this world, come home to your Self and heal the perceptions that have clouded your vision. Set yourself free from all fear and judgement. Do not fear for Mother Earth – simply love her. Do not judge those you have perceived as uncaring or destructive – simply love them. For the planet does not need to be defended but only loved. Once you are liberated from the confines of your false perceptions, the power of your Love will be unlimited. It will have the ability to create miracles of healing.

When you pluck a flower from the stem of a plant, do you appreciate the living organism that has brought this flower into being? When an animal is killed for food or for your pleasure, do you honour the consciousness of the one that has died? When you cut down a mighty tree for building materials or because it stands in the way of a planned construction, do you give thanks to the one whose life in this world has ended that your desires might be fulfilled?

I ask you this to encourage you to see beyond your own limited perspective into the heart of the Love that is present in all things. All of Creation is conscious and worthy of your love and your reverence. If Love is to find expression in the new world, all life must be valued and honoured. It matters not so much what you do, but why you do it. Whatever you decide to do, do it with love in your heart, honouring and respecting all life, all the expressions of the Presence of the Father.

When you act under the impetus of Love, you will accomplish far more in this dream world than you could ever hope to achieve by acting wilfully, reactively and defensively. Remember that all you see is your projection. When you dwell on this, you will realise that you have no other choice than to extend Love to all.

You are responsible for all you experience in this world. To respond to any events with anything other than Love is insane. And the ego is insane. It is convinced of its own power and wisdom and is not able to detect the error of its perceptions. To heal the mind, you must realise that the ego with which you have identified has no reality. You must look beyond the ego into the depths of silence within to realise the Truth of who you are.

Feel the depth of your bond with Mother Earth and love her. Do not fight for her but honour her and all life on this planet. All are aspects of your Self. All are the expression of Love in form. All are worthy of your love and your care. Love the soils and the sands of Mother Earth. Love her mountains and her rivers. Love and care for the plants that emerge from her soils and the creatures that roam over her lands. Love the sunlight that brings warmth and nourishment to her children. Love the rains that bring sweet moisture to slake her thirst. Include all in the sphere of your Love. When you love all wholeheartedly, this love will be returned to you a hundredfold.

Let us now for a time return to the forest in which we walked together. Feel again the stillness that pervades it. Sense the weight of your feet upon the fallen leaves as you take each step forward. Be aware of the life-force within these trees, your brothers. This glade is a sacred place. It is a haven of peace. It is a cathedral of Love. It awaits you here in the quietness of your mind to greet you when you would seek its serenity. This forest is a representation of all the quiet and sacred places found in the natural world. Seek out these places as often as you can and rest in them, for here you will find peace. Here you can realise your Oneness with all life. Here you will find your Self. Here you will discover the Presence of God.

Oneness

Precious friends, I join with you now to share the Love that unites our hearts together as One. For indeed we are One, One in Christ, inseparable from our Father. Feel my love, as a child will feel the deep love of his mother as she rocks him in her arms. If you still think of me as a being apart from you, know that we are ever One – One in all aspects of Divinity. One in Love, One in God, One in Truth.

Embrace the Oneness of all life. You are never alone, never apart from the Father. It is in acknowledging our Oneness in God that freedom is attained. You are eternally One with us all. Not separate, not alone. Never alone. Do you not see that it is the belief in separation that has led to all the chaos and confusion, the suffering and the dramas? We wish to promote within you now an absolute trust in all that is, and a certainty in what is true about you.

Find your comfort in the Oneness of all life, knowing that you are an essential part of the great wonder that the Father has brought forth. Awakening from the dream of separation is the goal of all, whether the goal is consciously chosen or otherwise. We ask you now to open more fully to the Truth of the Kingdom, to your Oneness with God, to your reality as an eternal spirit, beautiful and powerful and divine. You are God. You are Love. You are Light. This is the truth of your being.

You are not the body, but this world of dreams has kept you enthralled with its dramas and challenges. You are so convinced that these things matter that you grieve when things seem to go wrong. You respond with a whole gamut of emotions that carry you through highs and lows of feeling. But nothing that happens in this world matters.

If you sit before your television screens, it makes no difference whether you watch a sitcom or the news of the world that you believe is real. It is all energy in motion, thoughts manifesting in the physical, moulded and shaped by your mind. It does not serve you to become lost in it. It is all a fabrication. What does it have to do with the Reality of who you are? Love is what you are.

When you rest in the stillness, knowing you are One with all life, there is no seeking, no loneliness, no fear. There is only peace and gratitude. If you are feeling lonely and in want of company, are you not seeking? And this seeking itself is the very antithesis of peace. This is another demonstration of the tactics of the ego to keep you trapped in separation. You keep wanting to confirm the reality of the dream, so you manifest ways to do this. But it is all self-deception.

Can you not live your life as you are, remembering the truth, remembering that you are God? I would have you turn your mind from the things of this dream world to the world of the spirit. Turn your mind towards your Creator. Have done with smallness and limitation. Embrace your reality as the only begotten Son of the Father, One with all life. I do not ask you to go out into your world preaching of love. You do not have to rescue the world. But you can rescue yourself: you can rescue yourself from illusions.

Much that appears unloving is taking place in many parts of your world. But I say to you: do not try to fix the dream but wake up from the dream. Do not feel anxious about the wars and suffering and confusion that you see on your television screens. How could

Chapter 23: Oneness

this possibly aid your brothers and sisters in those places where this occurs? You believe you should be compassionate, but your fear and anxiety will only add to the confused energies playing out there. You need not strive to be loving towards those you judge to be the aggressors. You cannot counterfeit love. Know that all minds are joined and what you are seeing is your projection. Remember that a dream remains a dream. Simply know that Love is what you are always.

All those who appear as victims of war are not victims. They have drawn to themselves all that they are experiencing. And you are One with them all. You are One with all life. You are One with the families struggling to deal with floods and droughts. You are One with the cattle whose flesh you consume. You are One with the trees that are cut down to build your houses. Yes, love and serve all, but do not believe in suffering. Do not take sides against supposed aggressors. In Truth all life on this planet is a manifestation of Love.

Let those who have chosen what appears to be painful paths walk through their experience. You do not have to save them. They do not need to be rescued. They remain innocent and the sovereign masters of their lives. The Truth of who you are, the Truth of who they are, is unchanging. All are expressions of God's Love on Earth. They are dreaming a dream of apparent madness, but it remains a dream. The spirit is eternal, beyond life and death, beyond suffering.

The more you dwell on the troubles portrayed by the media, the more you worry about them, the more you fear them, the more the energies of discord are inflamed. You will do more to aid world peace by being at peace yourself, by speaking of peace, by living in peace moment to moment. You now stand at a critical point in the evolution of mankind. Will you give way to fear, or will you rise above the dramas and abide in peace?

How often have I advised you to practise allowance? Do not resist anything. Do not defend what does not need defending.

Remember that only Love is real, only Love heals and only Love transcends all things. You cannot allow fear to overwhelm you and imagine your choices will be healing. Remember the Truth. There is nothing wrong. There is no good or bad. There are no accidents in Creation. There is only Love, and Love abides at peace, in joy, eternally One with all life.

Beloved friends, the time of peace is now. Peace be unto you and all the brothers and sisters who populate this planet. Do not look outside of you to find peace because it is ever within. Do not ask warring countries to cease hostilities. Rather look within and quell the wars within you. There is nothing outside of you. You are *it*. Cease looking upon the troubles of the world as if they are outside of you. Look within, and know you are the All of everything.

You are not separate, not apart from all that you perceive. The world you see is your projection, and because this is so, you have the power to support its healing. While you stay lingering in this dream world, you believe that you are not responsible for all of it. But in Truth you are. If you come to recognise that you are One with your God, One with all life, One with the planet, you will know that you are mighty. You are powerful because you were born of Love, and Love is all that you are.

We have urged you to be in allowance and surrender all seeming problems, all concerns, to us. Continue to do this in every moment but recognise that, even as you surrender, you are One with all of us. Do not think this is contradictory. You can forgive all and love all and so create peace within so that you can begin to see it out in the world. Be not troubled by the illusion of war and discord and the threats of retaliation. Remember – it is all within you. You are not apart from any of it. Embrace your power and glory as the One. Celebrate your divinity and support the healing of the world by discovering the deep peace within you. Do not shy away from this. Own your power and your grace. Own the great depths of Love within you. No force can defeat the power of Love.

We have reminded you of the Oneness of all creation, but until it becomes your living reality it will remain a concept in the mind. When you come to know and feel in the depths of your being that you are not separate and alone, you will relinquish the false sense of self. You will embrace the truth that there is only One. It is no small thing to stand naked before your Father, free of all the shadowy costumes the ego wears. It is no small thing to commit your life totally to fulfilling the Will of the Father and let the grace stream of His Love carry you homewards.

The clouds of the old world have not yet fully dispersed, but this dispersion is assured. The threads of change have been woven into the tapestry of Creation. Love is on the ascendence and is exerting its power and grace in the hearts and minds of mankind. Give up the last traces of self-judgement and accept what is true about you. You are free and unlimited. You are divine. You live and breathe by the grace of God who lives and breathes as you. There is only One, and you are that One.

Freedom

Beloved children of God, we come again to remind you that the Truth of who you are is far greater than this body you seem to inhabit. You are infinite and eternal, and in this moment of time you function in many dimensions. When you look about you, you may feel helpless because you can seem to be trapped in a world that is out of control, a world of war and pain and dysfunctional relationships. It may appear that you cannot escape this.

There are times when you have known joy and there are times when you have experienced suffering, but always because you have drawn this to yourself. Many times, you have felt caught up in a world of darkness, of disorder, of the insanity of man's inhumanity to man. But never – *never* – have you been trapped in any experience. Even if you were caged in a dark, dank cell in the most formidable penitentiary, you still have freedom of mind. Though the body may be confined, your spirit, the Truth of who you are, can never be confined. If you feel small and alone and anxious, know that you always have the freedom of mind to go beyond all thought of fear and limitation. Never are you alone and never are you without the power to escape the constraints of egoic thinking by choosing anew to set yourself free to fly.

The Truth of who you are cannot be confined. We continue to remind you that you are pure consciousness. You are boundless and free. What will it take to convince you to embrace this truth about yourself? When will you be willing to give up your attachment to the ego's perceptions? The ego can be equated with suffering and limitation, and in Truth it has no reality. It is only the conditioned mind that believes in the stories of suffering and victimhood and clings to its conviction that it is small and limited. You are not the ego, nor have you ever been the ego. You are free and without boundaries, and the power of God lies within you.

Freedom is your birthright. You do not need to seek it. It resides within you now. And what is freedom? It is liberation from all fear. It is liberation from guilt and self-judgement – and all forms of judgement are self-judgement. No one and no thing can imprison the mind. In every moment you can reclaim your freedom by remembering the Truth of who you are.

We have called on you to be the Light of Christ. We have asked you to acknowledge the power and grace of your Being. You are indeed powerful, and your power arises not from struggling to achieve or from any attempts to control or manipulate your world. It arises when you recognise that the Father lives in you, as you. The freedom that you experience when you live as the Christ that you are is the natural outcome of the abandonment of all fear and the embracing of the Father's Presence within you.

If you allow yourself to be unwillingly controlled by the dictates of the society in which you live, you do so not because you lacked freedom but because you have forgotten who you are. Freedom stands side by side with integrity. The one who is true to herself is free. The one who fears the opinions or actions of another is confused and their fears are controlling them, not anyone or anything outside of them.

Look honestly at your life and observe where you give precedence to that which adheres to the rules of the society in which you live. Look well and recognise where you are conforming

Chapter 24: Freedom

to expectations and where you are truly acting mindfully and meaningfully, with integrity. How can you claim to be truly free if you fear disapproval or ostracism if you step outside of your society's proclaimed standards or conventions? How can you claim to be truly free if you allow others to manipulate or control you because you fear their criticism or rejection? How can you claim to be truly free if fears for your safety and security are guiding your choices?

Trust in the Truth of who you are and go beyond the small confines of the conditioned mind. You do not have to strive or strain to live. You have only to allow all to be as it is and trust in all that unfolds before you. You rest in the gentle arms of a God of great love. You need not look beyond your Self or this moment to discover this presence.

The question I encourage you to ask is 'Who am I?' Who are you really? Do you sense that the Truth of who you are is unchanging? Indeed, you are eternal and changeless. Can you be a body when this physical structure changes over time and ultimately dies? If you are not this thing that disintegrates back into the earth, then who are you? It is not enough for another to tell you that you are pure spirit, you must become deeply aware of this for yourself.

As you rest in the quiet, look silently upon the vagaries of the mind. Thoughts come and go. Sometimes they linger, at times they are fleeting. They are insubstantial. Realise that you are not your thoughts. What is this thing called 'mind'? Is it just a receiving station or does it emanate thoughts? Thoughts have power. They create experience, carrying you from one event to another. But you are not these things. If you touch your scalp, it seems solid, but could this be just a trick of the mind, convincing you that a dream is real? Could it be that the world you see with the physical eyes is just a product of consensus beliefs? Just as you are taught to eat your food and cleanse the body, could it be that the bed you lie on, the chair on which you rest, are just thought forms in which you have come to believe? I do not offer you answers to these questions. You must go inside yourself and seek the answers within. I come to you as your teacher and your friend, but I cannot decide for you what you will choose to believe. You must go within, into the depths of your being, and you will find all that you seek.

This mysterious thing called 'mind' is powerful. It can carry you beyond this world and lead you onwards into new lives and new experiences. In your mind you can travel across oceans and over mountains and sense the thoughts and emotions of another far away, not simply in this world but in other spheres. You can travel far and wide, or you can stay within the confines of the body and this place you see and experience now. This is the freedom you possess, and no one can rob you of this. It is your very nature, and you can use this freedom wisely to be of service and support the atonement. The mind is indeed powerful, but you are not the mind and have been deceived into thinking that the thoughts that parade through the mind are true.

Let us return to that question "Who am I?" Who are you in Reality? You are aware of a sense of self. When you speak the words "I am", you are acknowledging your living presence, but who is this "I" of whom you speak? You are not the name that was bestowed on you when you entered this world. You are not the changing form that the body adopted during this lifetime. You are not any of the many roles you undertook while here in this world. So, who is this "I"? As you continue to rest with this question, you will become aware of a spaciousness, an emptiness that is alive with consciousness.

Beyond the mind, beyond the body, there is no separate self. The concepts of "me" and "my" are learned concepts, an invention of mind, and you would be wise to question them. The conviction you hold of the "I" as a separate identity is an illusion of mind. You are not separate from the One, not separate from the All, not

Chapter 24: Freedom

separate from the great mystery that is God. The mind is confused and yet you turn to the mind for the answers you seek. You are not the mind, and the mind cannot inform you of what it does not know. When I ask you to rest with this question, I am asking you to go beyond mind into the depths of awareness that is the Truth of who you are. Do not seek for the answer where it is not. When you have rested with this question and come to realise that you are simply awareness itself, that you are indeed pure consciousness, you will realise that you are truly limitless and free, and that you have always been limitless and free.

Beloved friends, freedom is your birthright. It is given unto you by the One who birthed you. It cannot be taken away from you, but it can be denied. You can believe yourself to be small and limited and helpless, but this remains a false belief and has no reality. Claim your freedom now. Claim your Christhood. Never allow false images in the mind to deceive you. Remember who you are in Truth. Remember your divinity, your power and your grace. Remember the great light that shines upon you and from within you. And remember that you are free.

In this dream world of drama and chaos, this world of suffering and bewilderment, you continue to shine. You shine as a bright star, radiant, brilliant, and glorious. Look about you now and recognise that even when the mind dwells upon the troubles that have beset your planet and its peoples, yet is this world a beautiful and mysterious place. Just as you shine, so you can feel the light, the warmth, the love that is radiating from everything your eyes rest upon.

Glory be to God! Glory be to the Great Spirit, the One, the Only. And glory be to you who represent the Divinity of the Father. You are that One, not separate, not alone, not apart from but one with the mystery and magnificence that is the Supreme Being, that is God. Dwell on this often and sense the truth that is spoken. Sense with wonder and joy the reality of who you are. Sense your beauty and your greatness. Sense the great light that shines within and from you. This does not make you 'special'. This truth is not a morsel to feed to a hungry ego, but it is the living reality of who you and your brothers and sisters are.

The Light of God is your light, your truth, your mystery. Put aside all doubts and uncertainties now. Embrace the Truth of who you are, and finally – finally – cast from you the false beliefs in separation and suffering. Beloved friends, you are free, wonderfully and magnificently free. This freedom is not something that you must seek or earn or strive for. It is your essence and your glory. Embrace it now, and do not turn away from the gifts of Love that it brings you. Live as that which you are. Live as the Divine Truth that you represent. And be happy, gloriously happy, shining the light of your being upon all who have failed to see the light shining within themselves.

A Sense of Wonder

Praise be to the God who birthed you! Praise be to God, the Father of the One Creation! And praise be to you, His precious children. Beloved brothers and sisters, I come to you now to remind you once again that only Love is real, and bid you be at peace at all times, no matter what is unfolding in this life you call your own. Simply choose to be at peace.

No situation calls for anything save Love. Love is everything. Love is the healer. Love comforts and nurtures. It blesses all and harms none. It sees no fault and passes no judgement. It holds no expectations and makes no demands. It simply loves. It allows all things and trusts all things. It enriches and brings joy. It is the answer to every question and every uncertainty. It sees no problems but only solutions. It is all you require and all you truly seek. It is everything. And because Love is what you are, you need only be that which you are, at any time and at all times.

Let the mind dwell upon the wonder that Love is. Know that joy and light abound in everything and everyone. The world you experience is a dream world, but because you are Love, you have the power to bring Love to it. Just as light shines away darkness, Love will shine away all fear. Thus, as it is in Heaven, so it will be on Earth. And now, as you walk through your dream world, remember that all is well and there is nothing wrong.

We do not ask you to deny the dream. Simply remember that is a dream. You are pure spirit. You are consciousness. You are Love Itself and you are divine. When you focus your awareness in this dream world, when you experience yourself walking the planet, you can bring the Love that you are to all that you see.

We encourage you now to appreciate this life you are experiencing and look upon it with awe and wonder. Know that it is a gift, a gift to experience, to enjoy, to celebrate. We do not ask you to struggle or suffer for some great cause. We ask that you be who you are in Truth and to shine your light out into the world. And can this not be a wonderous joy? Can you appreciate how rich and fulfilling this can be?

Can you begin to think of this life you are experiencing as a wonderful adventure? Yes, wonderful. Full of wonder. You walk in a dream, but let it be a happy dream, a dream where you can experience playfulness and laughter. Not a weighty experience but one that uplifts and lightens the heart. We have suggested that you do not seek to change your world but to change your mind about the world and recognise that the essence of Love abides in everything in your world, in every event, in every situation.

We are not asking you to control your life. As you continue to practise allowance, we ask you to become open, open to living life more fully, to trust in the sacred interplay of energies at work on this planet. Have we not told you that joy is the natural state of mind of the one who has recognised that separation never occurred? Your Father's Will for you is perfect happiness. When we suggest that you be open to living life more fully, know that this is not a doing but an undoing. It is about demolishing the structures of thought the ego has created to protect itself from non-existent dangers.

So, we are encouraging you, as you move through this dream world, to live life fully, to break away from the old habits that have defined your behaviour for long periods of time. Such habits are not

Chapter 25: A Sense of Wonder

wrong. There is nothing wrong and all events are neutral. We are urging you to become open to a new way of living in this world. Be willing to explore the unknown. To hike new trails. To meet new friends. To taste foods previously untasted. To travel new highways. To climb hills you have never climbed. To explore unusual creative outlets. Become eager to question long-standing habits that you have been performing unthinkingly and look about you with fresh eyes. When actions are habitually performed without thought or meaning you remain in a prison of conformity that limits you and the expression of Love that you are.

Remember always that you are pure consciousness and are eternal and unlimited forever. So, question whether some of your regular habits have become limiting and stifling. Beware of the 'comfort zone' when it curbs your expression of who you truly are. Set yourself free within the dream to live each day anew. Let your days be enriched with freshness and aliveness and wonder. Respond to each moment with spontaneity, like an innocent child who looks upon the world without the weary weight of expectations and demands. Can you not see that you have chosen conformity to ensure your safety? This longing for safety and security limits you and weakens you. You are a free spirit, limitless and unbound by anything or anyone. Do not place limitations on the limitless or bind yourself to rigid habits that confine you. Be ever willing to travel new paths, taste new experiences and open your heart to ever greater ways to extend the Love that you are.

Set yourself free of all that restrains you now and live spontaneously and joyfully, with a deep appreciation of the possibilities presented by each moment you experience. While we continue to counsel you to be in allowance, this does not mean being in denial of the potential you hold to live this life you are experiencing more fully. Joy and fulfilment do not come by restricting yourself. They are born when you are willing to face your fears and be open to all that Life is offering you, to know the fullness of Love.

Do you think the regularity of your life makes your days easier and more comfortable? Or is the absence of spontaneity robbing you of the richness of seeing beyond the projections of the ego? Step out into each moment fearlessly and joyfully, with an eagerness of mind that appreciates the wonder and potential of the present moment. To be fully awake to this moment, to greet each fresh experience with innocence and spontaneity and a sense of wonder: this is to truly live.

Life is a precious gift. You came into this world eagerly, willingly embracing the circumstances of your birth and the family into which you were born. I am asking you now to reclaim the sense of wonder that you experienced at that moment. I am asking you to appreciate the value of your life on this planet. No matter what dramas you may have lived through, or what lies ahead in the many tomorrows you will face, recognise in each moment, with every breath you take, that your life is infinitely precious. It is divine. It is a living expression of the Love that the Father is.

Stop and look about you with a sense of wonder now. Let your awareness move from one object to another. Dwell on the Great Mystery that brought you here, into the awareness of this holy moment, into this place, into all that is here and now. How has it all come into manifestation? What wondrous forces of Nature have brought these things you see before you into being? Everything you see is alive with Love and consciousness. Everything is the sacred expression of God's Love in form. How miraculous is this! Here there are no ordinary things, no dead things, no insignificant things. All is precious. All is divine. All is alive with Love.

Look upon your world with great love. Look upon it with a sense of wonder, in awe at the great mystery that has brought forth all that you see before you. Treasure it. When you step out of your old patterns of behaviour and allow yourself to see your world anew,

Chapter 25: A Sense of Wonder

you will appreciate how embedded your thoughts have been in the past. Let not the past dictate how you relate to your world. Let it not deny the great Love that is being expressed in all that you see before you now. Rejoice in what is, not because you gain by doing so, not because it gives you earthly pleasure, but because it is the outpouring of the Father's Love that gives it life.

Take up any item you see before you. Hold it with respect. Recognise the Love that has brought it into manifestation in this world. It is a sacred object, worthy of your appreciation. When we do this often during your days, you will develop a growing sense of awe and wonder for all that is. Let the awareness of this object you hold now uplift your spirits and awaken a new veneration for the divinity in all things. This is not a trivial exercise. It is a movement towards seeing clearly with the eyes of Christ. It is a movement away from illusion towards the Truth of the Kingdom.

Do not separate yourself from this vision: acknowledge your divinity, the wonder of your Being, the beauty of your Presence. When you let go of all judgement of yourself and rest in the stillness of this moment, you can sense the holiness that is your true nature. This realisation comes when you go beyond thinking, when you simply open to what is present within you always. As you quieten the busy thoughts of the mind and rest quietly in the stillness, the awareness of Being will wash through you and bring peace to the soul. This peace is not born out of struggle or striving but simply by being still and allowing the Truth of who you are to rise in your awareness.

Beloved friends, so often have we reminded you of the Truth of who you are. We have reminded you of your divinity and the beauty of your soul. But when will you allow yourself to fully embrace this Truth? When will you say 'Enough!' to the illusion of smallness and limitation to which you have clung? When will you weary of the suffering and the dramas, and turn towards the peace that is your true state of mind? If you confront the actuality of your attachment to suffering, you will see your way out of the darkness that has clouded your vision.

We ask only that you stay centred in your journey and let Love be the motivation that causes you to act and speak. Let Love, not fear, be the guiding light that draws you onwards and upwards. When Love is the banner that you wave to the world, you will know that peace of mind, that trust, that quiet certainty that is the bounty that is gifted to all God's children who live in harmony with the Truth of the Kingdom.

Become alive to the beauty and wonder and infinite possibilities of this moment now. This precious moment holds within it the whole of eternity. Only in the present moment can you know freedom from the illusions that your belief in time has brought forth. Only in the present moment can you appreciate the beauty of this world before you, and glory in the bounty it is offering you. Only in the now can you realise that nothing is impinging upon you. There is no stern God frowning down upon you in great seriousness dictating to you what you should do or not do. The Father's Love is not conditional, and everything speaks of the Reality of His Love.

You are here on this planet by your own choice. No one forced you to come here. The family you entered was of your own choosing, and you knew why you came to be part of it. You came into this dream world for experience, and every experience was valuable: the fear and suffering, the joy and the laughter. Every event was chosen by you, for you. Every fear, every wound has been a call to yourself to awaken to the Reality of the wonder and joy of Love.

Nothing in Truth can limit the Holy Child of God. When you fully embrace the truth of who you are, you will realise that you too could walk on water, heal the sick and materialise objects before you. Do not struggle to acquire these abilities: this is not an exercise to enhance the ego's sense of self. They are simply a natural outcome of the recognition of the Truth. As your vibration rises you will know that you cannot be limited by thoughts in the mind. You cannot be diminished by the cultural beliefs of the society in which you live. No matter what beliefs you have been exposed to during your sojourn on planet Earth, these remain just thoughts in the mind and can be recognised as the false concepts of an ego still seeking to maintain control of its world.

Set yourself free of *all* beliefs. Old limiting beliefs must be cast aside without hesitation. And how do you do that when they seem so entrenched? By willingly, joyfully, remembering the Truth. See beyond the thought system that the culture you were born into has declared to be valid. You are a free spirit and can embrace mastery by setting yourself free of all that has imprisoned you previously. Acknowledge how deluded your beliefs have been and how they have limited you. Recognise that you have the power *now* to live as the master that you truly are. Beloved friends, it is time to go beyond time and space and live as the Christ that you are.

Now, as you go about your day, look upon the world with eyes of wonder, and remember the one relationship which is supreme. This is your relationship with your God. Acknowledge with awe the greatness of this One who is the Light of your life. This One is the essence of your being. This One is your strength, your wisdom and the great power of your love. This One is your Self. Know that this One loves you beyond your imaginings and is ever with you, inseparable from who you are. This One is your Life.

Truth Is

Beloved friends, Truth is. It does not need to be defended. It cannot be explained or analysed. Simply, Truth is. So, all the discussions, all the studying, all the interpreting – what does it do? Does it achieve anything? If it brings you fulfilment, if it brings you joy, then know it has some purpose. But do not try to extract Truth from the books you read or the teachers you listen to.

Simply, Truth is. The Real cannot be threatened. It shines forth as a radiant star: bright, eternal, unchanging and radiant with Love. You exemplify the Truth. Your brothers and sisters exemplify the Truth. The rising sun and the dew drop on a blade of grass exemplify the Truth. Give up all your attempts to grasp at the Truth. Give up struggling to understand. Cease to listen to the thoughts of the mind that would have you know the Truth.

Do not feel you need to understand, to interpret, to discuss or to question. The time for such diversions has passed. Now is the time to simply *be*, be who you are in Truth, and you are Love. You do not need to demonstrate this to others, or even to yourself. You are Love - without trying, without being concerned about the opinions of others, without striving to prove this to yourself in any way. When you are fully aware of who you are as the Christ, your very presence will be a light in the darkness, the evidence of Truth in the face of illusion.

Do not be concerned with words. Words can only point towards the Truth, but in themselves they are not the Truth. The concept of a chair is but a concept. It is not the chair. The concept of the world is but a concept. It is not the world. Everything you see is reflecting back to you the Love of the Father. All you see before you is a creation of mind, but the essence of all you see is Love. And only Love is real.

When you see an image, a shape or colour, or hear a sound, it has no reality. Because the essence of who you are is Love, you are real, and you project this Love out into all that you see. You are the creator of your experience, but you did not create the Love that you are. The imagined world that you have dreamt up can be blessed by the presence of Love. As you radiate the Love that you are out into the world you see, you bless it with the Love that the Father is. Thus, do you bring Heaven to Earth.

Beloved brothers and sisters, do not struggle with concepts now. What is more important: to be the presence of Love or to discuss the nature of the world? To shine the light of the Father's Love upon all that you see, or to struggle with concepts and ideas? To use the mind to question and analyse or to extend Love from the heart out into the world? Indeed, the script is written, and the time of your awakening is set, but you can know the Peace of God now. For peace is ever at rest in the depths of your being, only awaiting the silence of stillness to reveal its presence to you.

Strive not to understand what the ego would fain discover but go beyond the ego into the depths of your being where Love shines forth in all its glory. You cannot find peace or wisdom in the mind, because they can only be discovered in the heart. Look out upon the world now with eyes of love and forgiveness, and let all things be just as they are. You need change nothing, nor strive for anything, nor seek anything. Love what is, and the peace that rests in the core of your being will find a home in your consciousness. Only Love is real. Images are not real. Concepts are not real. Thoughts are not real. There can be no confusion when you accept the simple truth – *only Love is real.*

Truth is, and there is nothing you need do, say or experience. Relinquish any belief that the world needs saving from itself. All is well now. Let all events you are aware of take place without hinderance. Do not judge them as wrong or harmful. Simply accept what is with love and compassion and humility. Do not mistake unworthiness and self-imposed restrictions for humility. Humility reveals to the world that you have nothing to prove, nothing to defend, nothing to fight for. Rather your humility will demonstrate your power and your presence, and your willingness to let go the demands of the world and fulfil the Will of God, wherever it leads you, whatever it asks of you.

Allow events to unfold without trying to control them in any way. This is the simplest, most relaxing, most peaceful course to take. There is nothing to do, nowhere to go, nothing to achieve. And what does this mean? Are you compelled to sit silently while the world passes you by? Indeed not. We have told you many times: follow your heart. Follow your bliss. Not as defined by the egoic mind, but by the deepest urgings of your soul. You have but to listen to the heart, to its wisdom, to its truth, to its subtleties. In the quietness of the heart lies all the answers you seek.

All the experiences you have known during this lifetime remain neutral events. They were chosen by you quite deliberately to set you free to know the God in all things. Does this sound contradictory? Why would you choose suffering or limitation when the Truth is shining before you in all you see? You do so within the dream so that you may expand your capacity to love.

It is easy to love when all is well – two lovers walking hand-in-hand along the seashore; a baby innocently exploring his world with joy and excitement; looking out upon a beautiful sunset; watching a majestic bird in flight. All such images bring a gentle smile to the face, and the heart feels light and free. What if you experience illness or see a brother aggressively attacking another, or look upon extreme poverty or the ruination of the life of a drug addict? Can you see God's Presence in such situations? Can you see God in the abusive alcoholic who beats his wife? Or the school yard bully who terrorises vulnerable and innocent students? Can you see it in the destruction of your forests or the pollution of your waterways?

There is only God, and the Presence of God can be recognised in everything, in every moment. Trust in what you see. Trust in the power of God that is allowing you to see and experience what you do. See beyond the pain and the disorder and the disharmony. There is nothing wrong. Trust not in some external God that is apart from you but the God who stands forth as the essence of your being. Know that your Father is ever present, in you, as you, looking through your eyes, caressing with your hand. And know that all is well.

The world you experience is a dream. It is created by thoughts and beliefs and expectations. When you experience suffering it is always by your own choice. Never are you a victim. You are simply dreaming that you are suffering. And you do so because you believe you will gain by experiencing suffering. We have told you that suffering is never necessary, and yet while you dream of separation, all manners of dramas and discord are experienced.

When you fully realise who you are in Truth, you will abandon all perception of the value or purpose of suffering. Only the ego suffers because it is convinced that suffering is possible. The awakening spirit can find peace beyond suffering because Love is the *only* thing that is real. You are the presence of Love. This is who you are always. Remember that the Father lives in you, as you, and through you.

Because Love is in your mind, it is present in all you project outwards. Even in the dream, Love is present because it is your

Chapter 26: Truth Is

dream, and you are Love. Thus, Love can be found in every situation and in every drama. There is only God, and there is nothing outside of God.

The ego may be convinced that it knows what is right, but the spirit rests quietly in the place of not knowing. It does not defend its opinions, because it accepts that Truth does not need to be defended or even defined. *Truth simply is.* If you partake in an argument and aggressively protest the rightness of your viewpoint, you risk losing sight of what is real. Abandon the need to be right because it separates and leads you away from peace. Opinions are just opinions and are always questionable.

Love is. God is. Truth is. Love, God, Truth: all are beyond time. Though you may struggle to find words in your language to define them, yet they are. They need no definition because they are beyond definition. You strive to understand them with the mind, but this is not the task of the mind. Nor is it possible for the mind to understand what is beyond its capabilities. The heart, however, does not need to struggle to understand, to analyse and interpret. The heart feels and trusts and allows.

Truth is beyond description because words always limit. You cannot contain the unlimited. You cannot package God. Give up trying to define what cannot be defined. Cease trying to understand the great mystery that God is. Rest quietly in not knowing. It is a peaceful place, a place blessed with Love and Light. It is offered to you always. Trust in God. Trust in the Truth. Trust in not knowing.

We ask nothing of you other than to be that which you are, and you are the Truth exemplified. Please, once and for all, give up your striving and your seeking. Give up struggling to understand. Give up *trying*. Have we not told you often enough that there is nothing you need to learn, nothing you need achieve, nothing you need become.

Stop right now. Here, in this moment, and know that you

are God incarnate. Rest in the stillness, without agendas, without expectations, and feel the Presence of God within you. Feel the Love that is within you and all about you. It is so simple. Rest in the quiet and just be what you are. Simply be. And know that you are the All of everything.

The Joy of Being

Beloved friends, when you look upon a beautiful sunset and your heart soars with joy, from whence comes this feeling? Does it lie inherent in the scene you see? Because nothing is outside of you, joy is not to be found outside of you. No set of conditions need exist for you to experience this happiness. Joy does not wait lurking in some splendid vision of material wealth. It does not rest in the arms of a lover. It does not inhere in the acquisition of a long-sought award or prize. It lies within you always. *Always.* When you seek outside of you for anything, you fail to see that you are the master of your wellbeing. You decide how you will feel in each moment.

You can deny this, or you can shirk your responsibility for your situation in life, for your attitude of mind and your feelings, but never is another soul or anything outside of you responsible for the feelings you are experiencing. You know this to be true, but how many times during the course of your days do you forget this, and fall into the old habit of projecting responsibility for how you feel outside yourself? Look well upon your own behaviour and do not deny the tendency to play the victim.

This is a world made manifest by the collective thoughts of all. The wars, the extremes of weather, the floods and the droughts, the fall of the stock exchange, the diseases that run rampant through your communities: none of this is outside of you. Do not rescind responsibility for all that occurs on your planet. Do not try to justify your projections. You are responsible because there is only One Creation, and you are that One. Do not separate yourself from All That Is. Embrace the truth of your Oneness with God and His Creation.

This responsibility need not weigh heavily upon you. Many times have I told you that all is well and there is nothing to fear. All the events manifesting on Mother Earth, all the suffering that you have dreamt up, all the discord and the disharmony, it remains an illusion of mind. It will all pass away. Only Love endures, and only Love can heal the aberrations created by the mind. The choice to love will guide you to question the thoughts leading you away from peace. Follow the wisdom of the Heart now. Face the responsibility for all that the mind has brought forth and acknowledge your power to rise out of the darkness that was but a dream.

Finally – *finally* – it is time to confront the truth. You are Love made manifest in form. You are powerful beyond measure. The confused mind has bewitched you into believing that an illusion was real, but a dream remains a dream. Embrace the freedom that was bequeathed to you by your Father. Awaken from the dream and accept that you are the Holy Child of God. In Truth no erroneous thoughts can limit you. No ancient sense of guilt can rob you of your innocence. No darkness can shut out the brilliance of your light. No dream of discord or suffering can deprive you of the joy of being.

This awakening to the Truth is simple. Do not believe that it must be complex, require great effort and be difficult to attain. When you accept the Truth of who you are, you will laugh at the absurdity of the thought of limitation. You will recognise that all that was required was the acknowledgement of your Oneness with the Father. Separation is identified as the lie that it is. How simple does living become! No longer need you struggle to achieve anything. No longer are you weighed down by guilt over the past. No longer need you devise great plans for the future because you are content to be totally present with what is. To feel the joy of being.

When not distracted by thoughts of the past or the future, you can become aware of the beauty and wonder of the present moment, and conscious of the great mystery and grace of the Father's Presence that is being expressed in all that you see. Joy arises spontaneously, not because you have sought it, not because you needed it, not because you wished to escape from world weariness and discontent. It arises because it is the natural state of mind of the one who has recognised the Truth and has embraced their Oneness with All That Is.

God is indeed great! And the Love that God is will ever triumph over darkness and delusion. When the prodigal son has returned home to his loving Father, no longer feeling alone and abandoned, the dread nightmare that had entrapped his mind will be no more. The shadows have dispersed, and the sun of the Father's Love is shining brightly, illuminating a world at peace with itself.

Joy is your natural state of being. When you are not feeling joyful, question what thoughts are impeding the passage of joy into your awareness. Come home to the Truth. Come home to peace. Experience the bliss of simply being. To be fully present to what is before you now, without resistance, without judgement, without fear in any form – this is the great wonder of Love being expressed through you. This is the joyous exemplification of the Father's Presence made manifest.

Sense the Love alive within you now. When you do, you will look upon the world with soft eyes, uplifted by a quiet happiness and a blissful expansiveness. There can then be no thought of problems or discord, no perception that there is something amiss. You see that all is well in your world, and it is filled with wonder, beauty and mystery. The joys of Creation lie before you. You have no cause, no impulse, to ask for anything other than this loveliness before you now, revealed in the simplest of things – a cup resting on a table, a single strand of hair mirroring sunlight, the patterns in the bark of a tree, the sound of a baby's cry. The beauty of Creation needs no embellishment. All is as it is and is wondrously beautiful.

To be present thus, quiet and content, asking no more from your God than this place, in this moment – this is Heaven. Beloved brothers and sisters, you cannot ask for a greater happiness than this – to abide fully in the Father's Presence, totally at One with His Creation. The world cannot offer you a richer experience. When your love of your Father fulfils you, what more could you ask for? Nothing. What more could you possibly need now? Nothing. The richness of the wondrous present is enough.

This joy of being is the joy of loving and allowing and surrendering unto the Father's Will. You can have no greater purpose; you can know no greater fulfilment than this. The great seriousness of this world does not serve you. Let the child within you emerge and embrace your innocence and playfulness. Feel the joy of the dance of life. As you grow increasingly conscious of the Truth of who you are, the wonder of the Father's Presence will be discovered in all that you see and hear. Let Love light up your eyes and bring a sweet smile to your visage. Rejoice in the awakening of God's children. Rejoice in the Truth of who you are and the great love that is alive in you now. Because you are the manifestation of the Father's Love, you have the power and wisdom to overcome all dreams of darkness and disorder.

This Love that is alive within you can heal this world and bring new life into what once seemed stricken and despairing. It is *you* who will be the saviour of this world. It is your love and your life that will restore balance and health to all. It is your recognition of Oneness that will teach others that they are not apart from the One Life, the One Creation, the One God. You will teach them that they can know peace once again and can feel the simple joy of being the

Chapter 27: The Joy of Being

Truth of who they are.

When you look about you and find great joy in simple things – in sunlight reflected on a body of water, in the scent of a blossoming rose, in the sound of leaves rustling in a breeze – remember that this joy is arising from within you. When you delight in the sound of children's laughter, know that this is because happiness is always residing in the innermost recesses of your being. When your spirit takes flight at the sight of a beautiful seascape, you can be sure that this freedom to soar always rests deep within you. The doubting, questioning, critical mind can be silenced, and you can choose to surrender to this moment, whatever it may bring you. You can transcend the small self and rise into the quiet happiness of being fully present to what is here and now.

Beloved friends, I love you and I know the reality of who you are. I see you as you respond to the ebbs and flows of your daily life. I am walking with you as you travel through these last days of this old world, a world that has been such a burden to the spirit of those who long for peace. Take my hand now and let not your steps falter as we move forward together through this final chapter of this ancient dream. Because I too have walked in human form upon your planet, I have known the suffering and the uncertainty that you have known. I understand you when your doubts arise, and you question the path you are following. I understand you when fear has taken a hold on your mind. And I understand you when you look with confusion upon a world at war with itself. But I also know the power of the love that rests in your heart. I know the strength and integrity that supports you. And I know the brilliance of the light that shines from within you.

Now you can stand before the world as a herald of the Truth. We do not ask you to deny what you perceive but look beyond what is seen by the physical eyes and see into the heart of things. Recognise that you look upon a dream world, a world that has no reality in Truth. When you view this world with eyes of love and a heart of compassion, you will be conscious of the Divine Light that is shining from within all that you behold.

You can be that beacon of light that illuminates the path of those seeking to find their way back to peace. You can rest at any time in the quiet and tranquil garden that lies within you always. You have the wisdom and the compassion to support the healing of those bewitched by fear who still believe themselves to be separate and alone. The warmth of your smile can bring comfort to weary souls. Your joy can be the instrument that awakens joy in others. Your laughter can uplift hearts weighed down by apprehension. You are powerful indeed when you act as the servant of the Divine.

Precious brothers and sisters, the time has come when you must reach into yourself – into the depths of your being – to find what answers you yet seek. In Truth you know all that you need to know now. I have nothing more to teach you. You do not need any more books, any more information, any more mystical experiences. You need only *live* what you know. You are everything, and yet you are no thing. You are the Holy Child of God, and your light shines out on the world as a radiant star. Be that star now. Live what you know. I can teach you nothing more: I can only reassure you and remind you of what you already know.

As the old world is passing away, our journey together continues. Never am I apart from you. Together we walk onwards towards the new world, a world of peace and happiness, a world where Love is in ascendence. This is a world that we will create together as One. Here you will experience the joy of being that is your birthright. Here you will know the Oneness of all Creation. And as you take your final footsteps into the Light, as the cords that bound you to the past fall away, a deep peace descends upon you and the great mystery that is the Mind of God embraces you. You have come home.

www.ingramcontent.com/pod-product-compliance
Lightning Source LLC
Chambersburg PA
CBHW061728070526
44583CB00024B/3044